ANTIOCH AND JERUSALEM

To Josepha and Michael, in love and admiration

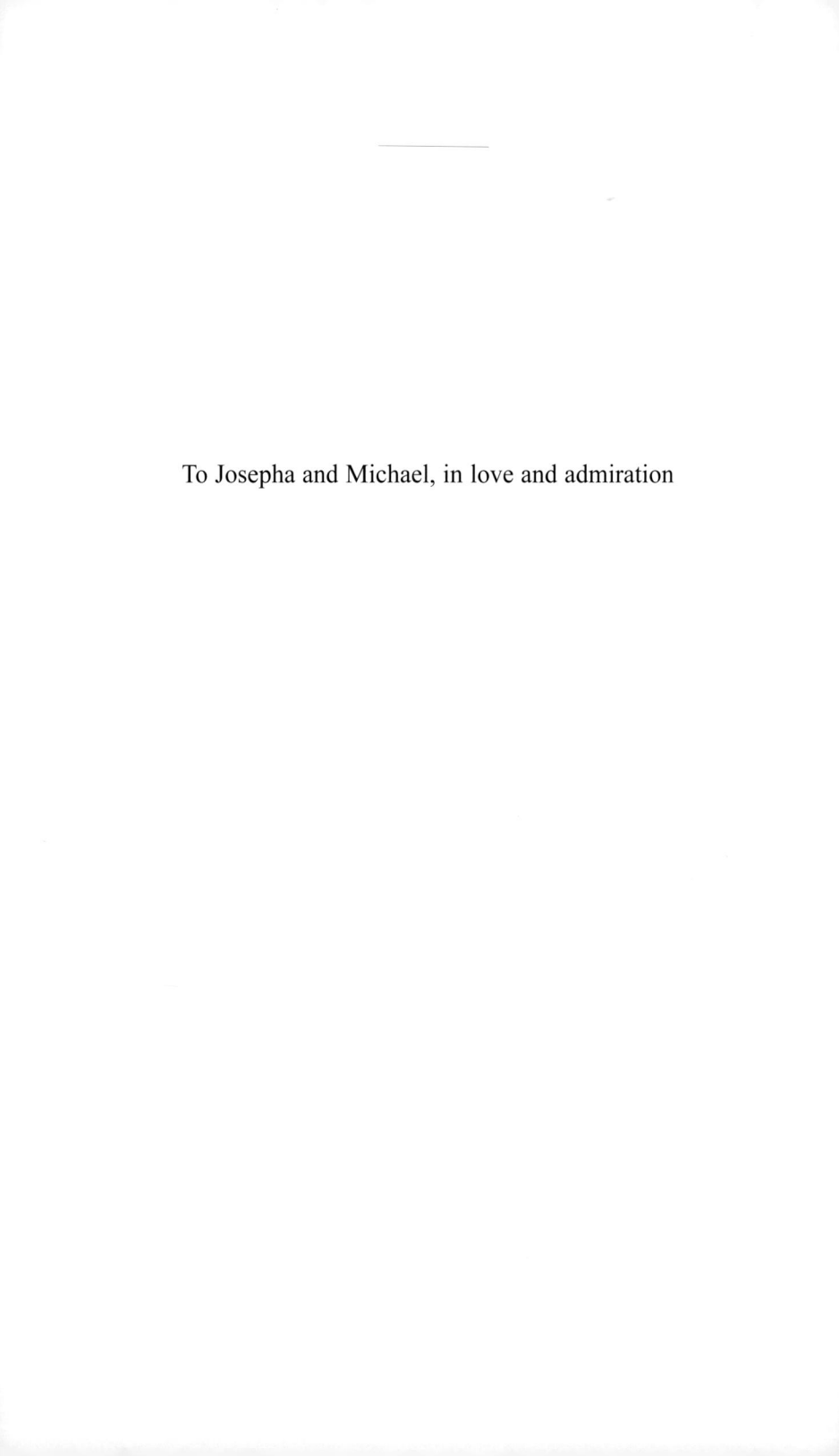

ANTIOCH AND JERUSALEM
THE SELEUCIDS AND MACCABEES IN COINS

DAVID M. JACOBSON

SPINK

© David M. Jacobson 2015

Typeset by Russell Whittle

Printed and bound in Malta
By Gutenberg Press Ltd.

for the publishers
Spink & Son Ltd., 69 Southampton Row
Bloomsbury, London, WC1B 4ET, UK

www.spink.com

All rights reserved. No part of this publication may
be reproduced, stored in a retrieval system or
transmitted in any form or by any means,
electronic, mechanical, photocopying, recording or
otherwise, without the prior permission of the
publishers.

ISBN 978-1-907427-54-1

CONTENTS

Preface. vii

CHAPTER 1
Introduction. 1

CHAPTER 2
The Legacy of Alexander the Great in the Southern Levant 11

CHAPTER 3
Antiochus III and Seleucus IV - the Prelude to the Maccabaean Rebellion. . . 19

CHAPTER 4.
Antiochus IV and the Outbreak of the Rebellion 33

CHAPTER 5.
From Antiochus V to Tryphon – The Wars of the Maccabees 49

CHAPTER 6.
From Antiochus VII to Antiochus IX – Consolidation of Hasmonaean Rule. . 83

CHAPTER 7.
From Seleucus VI to Antiochus XII – Disintegration of the
Seleucid Kingdom and Establishment of the Hasmonaean Monarchy. 101

CHAPTER 8.
The Extinction of the Seleucid Kingdom and Subsequent Developments . . . 123

APPENDIX.
Greek, Roman and Jewish Sources Cited 137

BIBLIOGRAPHY 153

STEMMATAS
Seleucids. 166
Maccabees/Hasmonaeans 167

PREFACE

Every December Jewish people around the world celebrate Hanukkah, a joyous holiday that commemorates the miracles related to the Jewish defeat of the forces of the Seleucid Syrian King Antiochus IV, who aggressively followed his predecessors' efforts to Hellenize the monotheistic Jews.

But the relationship between the Maccabees of Judaea and the Seleucids of Antioch is more complicated and intertwined than the simple story of Hanukkah.

In this short but significant volume, David Jacobson tells the story of this relationship in detail. While other historians have tended to lean almost exclusively on the text of the books of the Maccabees (not canonized in Judaism) or Flavius Josephus, Jacobson gathers all of the primary sources. In other words, he includes information from many other ancient documents and mixes carefully with crucial data from archaeology, ancient inscriptions, and especially Jacobson's speciality, coins. These are all illustrated with magnificent colour photographs.

Previous detailed histories of this period—roughly 150 years—between the reigns of Antiochus III and Antiochus XII have mostly ignored the evidence of the coins. This is partly because many of the histories were written before a great deal of relatively recent (in the last 100 years or so) numismatic scholarship. But it is also because many historians simply ignored the information provided by the coins because they neither knew about them nor took the time to understand their significance.

The story Jacobson brings us is not limited to Seleucids and Jews, but includes Parthians, Armenians, Nabataeans, among others, and eventually leads us, in a nicely explained cause-and-effect manner, to the Roman domination of Judaea.

The coins, Jacobson notes, accurately illustrate how the rulers of the time "wanted to be seen by their subjects and the world at large."

Jacobson uses the contemporary coins at every turn in his story. Thus we can see the faces of the kings of the Seleucid dynasty, and understand how their Greek names and titles reflected their personalities as they wished their subjects and their foes to see them. On the other hand, the Jews of the time banned graven images from their coins, and these provide us with a different basis of information including, by the way, graphic illustrations of how most of the Maccabean coin designs copied earlier Seleucid motifs.

In short this is the fascinating story of how the Seleucid successors of Alexander III (the Great) at first dominated their geography, and later fragmented it—as Jacobson shows us the Seleucids suffered 17 kings, a queen, and an autocrat in a century and a half, and in just under a century the Judean Jews had six Maccabean rulers.

Some readers will be surprised to learn that the Jewish victory against Antiochus IV did not sever relationships between the Seleucids and the Maccabees which continued to range from near suzerainty to alliance and in between. Jacobson further helps us understand how this tumultuous relationship eventually led to the downfall of the Maccabean (Hasmonean) Dynasty and the subjugation of Judaea to Rome, beginning in 64 BCE when Pompey the Great led his troops to Syria and eventually conquered Jerusalem.

In 40 BCE the Roman Senate named Herod I (the Great) as King of the Jews. On the ground in Jerusalem, however, Mattathias Antigonus, the last Maccabean ruler still reigned as King and High Priest. By 37 BCE however, Herod I, supported by Roman forces, defeated Mattathias Antigonus and his Parthian supporters. As a result, the Seleucid-linked Hasmonean Dynasty was replaced with the Roman-dominated Herodian Dynasty. However, elements of the Seleucid legacy relating to the administrative structure, currency system and architectural tradition lived on in Judaea for another century or so.

David Hendin
American Numismatic Society

CHAPTER 1

INTRODUCTION

At around the time that a large part of humanity celebrates Christmas, Jews commemorate Hanukkah. It is an eight day festival, starting on the 25th day of Kislev according to the Hebrew calendar. The name 'Hanukkah' derives from the Hebrew verb חנך, meaning "to dedicate" (the altar) [cf. 1 Macc. 4.56]. The festival is not mentioned in the Hebrew Bible, but the historical event that it recalls is preserved in the books of 1 and 2 Maccabees, composed by Jewish authors in antiquity, and preserved only in Greek and not recognised as part of the Jewish canon. A letter sent in SE 188 (125/4 BCE) by the Jews of Jerusalem to their coreligionists in Egypt enjoining them to observe Hanukkah as an annual eight day festival has come down to us in 2 Maccabees [1.1-10]. There, it is described as "a Festival of Tabernacles in the month of Kislev", no doubt to mark the fact that the celebration of that festival in 164 BCE had to be deferred until the Temple could be purified of the profanation that it had suffered and its devotees could leave their hiding places and resume their worship of the one God [2 Macc. 10.5-8]. But what was this episode actually about?

In Jewish tradition, Hanukkah is specifically associated with a miracle, explained as follows in the Babylonian Talmud and written six centuries after the event:

> "For when the Greeks entered the Temple, they defiled all the oils therein, and when the Hasmonaean dynasty prevailed against and defeated them, they made search and found only one cruse of oil which lay with the seal of the High Priest, but which contained sufficient for one day's lighting only; yet a miracle was wrought therein and they lit (the lamp) therewith for eight days" [Babylonian Talmud, *Shabbat* 21b].

This account of miraculously preserved oil is not too dissimilar from an episode related in 2 Maccabees 1.19-2.3, but in connection with Nehemiah's attempt to restore Temple sacrifice after the return of the Jews from exile in Babylon. In a search for altar fire hidden by priests at the behest of Jeremiah when the First Temple was destroyed, their descendants came upon some purifying oil, that had laid hidden, and used it to light the sacrificial altar. It is easy to see how this story might have morphed into the later account of the miracle of Hanukkah.

A sentence is added in the daily synagogue prayers during Hanukkah referring to the victory achieved over the Syrians by Mattathias and his sons, an event that enabled the Temple to be repossessed and cleansed. In Pharisaic circles the political achievements of the Hasmonaeans, the descendants of Mattathias (the dynasty being named after the great grandfather of Mattathias, *Asamonaios* in Greek [Josephus, *AJ* 12.265] or *Hašmonai* in Hebrew, according to rabbinic literature), were pushed into the background, and the very name of Judah the Maccabee (Judas Maccabaeus) got largely forgotten by Jews. Their adversaries were referred to as "Greeks" or "Syrians" and there was no mention of the kingdom involved, let alone the fact that the recovery of the Temple was but one episode in a long drawn-out struggle by the Maccabees to wrest full independence from Seleucid domination.

The 1st century CE Jewish historian, Flavius Josephus, provides a more rational account of the origin of what he calls the "Festival of Lights":

> "And so Judas together with his fellow-citizens celebrated the restoration of sacrifices in the temple for eight days, omitting no form of pleasure, but feasting them on costly and splendid sacrifices, and while honouring God with songs of praise and the playing of harps, at the same time delighted them. So much pleasure did they find in the renewal of their customs and in unexpectedly obtaining the right to have their own service after so long a time that they made a law that their descendants should celebrate the restoration of the temple service for eight days. And from that time to the present we observe this festival, which we call the festival of Lights, giving this name to it, I think, from the fact that the right to worship appeared to us at a time when we hardly dared hope for it" [Josephus, *AJ* 12.323-325; translated by Ralph Marcus].

Hanukkah as such is first mentioned in St. John's gospel, where it is stated that Jesus was at the Jerusalem Temple during "the Feast of Dedication (of the altar) and it was winter" [John 10.22–23]. The Roman Catholic Church, which includes 1 and 2 Maccabees among its canonical scriptures, assigns August 1st as the feast day to commemorate the Maccabees. The Eastern Orthodox Church celebrates the Holy Maccabaean Martyrs on August 1st, the first day of the Dormition Fast. These martyrs are not the actual Maccabees, but rather the mother (unnamed in 2 Maccabees, although named variously Miriam bat Tanhum in rabbinical sources and Hannah in popular accounts), and her seven sons who preferred martyrdom to relinquishing their faith; they are described as follows:

"Shortly before the Maccabaean revolt, Antiochus IV Epiphanes arrested a mother and her seven sons, and tried to force them to eat pork. When they refused, he tortured and killed the sons one by one. The narrator mentions that the mother "was the most remarkable of all, and deserves to be remembered with special honour. She watched her seven sons die in the space of a single day, yet she bore it bravely because she put her trust in the Lord" [2 Macc. 7.20; New English Bible translation].

Each of the sons made a speech as he died, and the last one remarked that his brothers "have now fallen in loyalty to God's covenant, after brief pain leading to eternal life" [2 Macc. 7.36]. The narrator ends by saying that the mother died, but not how. This is the earliest recorded account of martyrdom for the sake of religious belief in Judaeo-Christian tradition.

Ill. 1.1. Hanukkah lamp (*Hanukkiah*) of the late Roman period, unearthed near Jerusalem, c. 1900

This publication offers a perspective of the history of the Seleucid kingdom, the Maccabees and their Hasmonaean successors from the vantage point of the coin evidence, spanning the reigns of the Seleucid king, Antiochus III, who seized possession of the southern Levant from the rivals of his dynasty, the Ptolemies, to Antiochus XII, a period of one and a half centuries. Ancient coins provide valuable and direct historical testimony, complementing information culled from textual sources and occasionally even filling important gaps in the historical record. Taken together, this rich body of evidence provides a remarkably detailed record of this important period in Jewish history.

All the same, many key ancient historical narratives have come down to us in fragmentary form, as noted in the Appendix summarising the principal Greek and Roman sources. Most of these also suffered alteration at the hands of later copyists. On the other hand, we have a reasonably comprehensive corpus of ancient coins which, being composed of durable metals (copper, silver and gold), are more durable than fragile parchment and papyrus, and they usually bear informative inscriptions naming the issuing authority, accompanied by poignant motifs – furnishing interesting snatches of historical information – and, of course, portraits of named rulers.

Ill. 1.2. Brass Hanukkah lamp (*Hanukkiah*), Netherlands, early 20th century

Whereas the modest fractional bronzes struck by the Hasmonaean rulers in Judaea are devoid of human images in deference to Jewish religious sensibilities in antiquity, the exceptionally fine portraiture of Seleucid kings on their coins allows us to glimpse something of their appearance, albeit idealised to a greater or lesser extent, and lifts them out of a narrative of faceless names. From these images, it is possible to discern something of their personalities, and they are especially telling about how they wanted to be seen by their subjects and the world at large, while the reverse motifs and Greek inscriptions, or coin legends, name them and say something about their religious affiliations and political outlook. Seleucid coins also allow us to better appreciate the increasing instability of the dynasty and disintegration of royal authority in the course of the 2nd century BCE, which enabled the Maccabaean revolt in tiny Judaea to succeed against the odds. Indeed, looking at the respective genealogies, in the years 164-76 BCE, there were just six members of the Hasmonaean family administering Judaea, while the Seleucid realm saw no less than 17 kings, a queen (the Egyptian Cleopatra Thea) and an autocrat (Tryphon) occupying the throne. One of the Seleucid kings, Demetrius II, had two separate reigns, the first between 146 and 138 BCE (terminated by a military defeat and his falling into Parthian captivity), and a second, shorter one, from 129 to 126/5 BCE, which ended no less abruptly with his murder at Tyre. The process of fragmentation of the Seleucid monarchy provided Rome with a ready opportunity to progressively sap Seleucid power and then gain mastery of the entire Levant.

The coins illustrated in this volume have largely been chosen from an anonymous collection. They bring to life the tempestuous sequence of events that gave birth to an independent Hasmonaean state. Often more than one example of a coin bearing the profile portrait of a Seleucid king is illustrated to highlight some of the variations in their representation, which range from somewhat realistic to idealised renditions.

Principal Ancient Sources Relating to Hanukkah:
1 Maccabees 4.56.
2 Maccabees 1.1-10; 10.5-8.
John 10.22–23.
Josephus, *Antiquitates Judaicae* (*AJ*) 12.323-325.
Mishnah, *Bikkurim* 1.6; *Rosh HaShanah* 1.3; *Ta'anit* 2.10; *Megillah* 3.4, 6; *Mo'ed Katan* 3.9; *Baba Kama* 6.6.
Babylonian Talmud, *Shabbat* 21b.

CHAPTER 2

THE LEGACY OF ALEXANDER THE GREAT IN THE SOUTHERN LEVANT

In a lightning military campaign from 333-331 BCE, the young Macedonian king, Alexander the Great, and his mobile Macedonian army swept through the Middle East, Egypt and then advanced eastwards to the western edge of India conquering the mighty Persian Empire. At the end of his short life, having not quite reached his 33rd birthday, Alexander was the unrivalled leader of the world that he knew before he set out. Through his stunning success, the political order that had been established by Cyrus the Great two centuries earlier was totally transformed. Gone was an oriental administration that used Aramaic as its official language and in its place was planted one from the West that conducted its governance and business in Greek.

The transition to Macedonian rule in the former Persian satrapy of Yehud (the Aramaic name for Judah), as far as can be ascertained, was a smooth one, and became enshrined in a legendary tale of a visit by Alexander to Jerusalem, where he was met by the splendidly attired Jewish High Priest, Jaddus, in Jerusalem and respectfully offered a sacrifice in the Temple [Josephus, *AJ* 11.326-339]. There, he was shown the Book of Daniel and recognised himself as the unnamed Greek who, according to prophesy, would destroy the Persian Empire [Dan. 8.21 – also according to the interpretation of this allegorical passage by Josephus, *AJ* 10.273]. Because chapters 7-12 of Daniel have been shown to have been written after

Ill. 2.1. **Alexander III 'The Great' (336-323 BCE). AR tetradrachm** (26 mm, 17.26 gm). Damascus mint, struck c.330-320 BCE. Head of a youthful Herakles, wearing a lion skin headdress / Zeus seated left on an ornamental throne, holding a long sceptre in his left hand and eagle in his right, with ΑΛΕΞΑΝΔΡΟΥ inscribed on the right; to the left, the forepart of a ram; above the struts of the throne, two dots; below bottom strut, ΔΑ. Price no. 3205.

Ill. 2.2. Lysimachus, Thrace (305-281 BCE). AR Tetradrachm (31 mm, 17.21 gm). Lampsacus mint. Struck 297/6-281 BCE. Diademed head of the deified Alexander / Athena, seated, holding a Nike with a wreath and accompanied by a spear and shield; herm to the outer left. ΑΞ monogram to the inner left. The Greek inscription reads [B]ΑΣΙΛΕΩΣ ΛΥΣΙΜΑΧΟΥ. Thompson *Lysimachus* no. 50; *SNG France* nos. 2553-4.

165 BCE, this detail, and probably the entire incident, is a later invention.

The initial Macedonian encounter with the Samaritans, an Israelite community claiming descent from the tribes of Menasseh and Ephraim and based in Samaria, was not so happy. The Samaritans, who established their rival temple on Mount Gerizim overlooking Shechem (Nablus), rebelled against the occupying Macedonian authority. A group of leading residents made a futile escape from Samaria, ending up as doomed fugitives in a hillside cave at Wadi Daliyeh, north of Jericho where their skeletons and a cache of accompanying legal and administrative papyri were found in recent times.

At his death, Alexander left behind an illegitimate and subnormal half-brother, Philip Arrhidaeus, and a widow, the Bactrian princess Roxane, who was carrying his unborn son, and there was no royal heir who was immediately capable of leading his vast empire. In those circumstances, it was only to be expected that his coterie of able Macedonian generals would split up and engage in a power struggle among themselves. Ptolemy took possession of Egypt and made the recently founded city of Alexandria near the Nile Delta his capital. By 320 BCE he had extended his control to Palestine and southern Syria. His first main rival was Antigonus *Monopthalmos* ("the one-eyed"). Other *Diadochi* (as these "successors" to Alexander were called) joined in the fray until a fairly stable division of territory was arrived at, following the battle of Ipsus (301 BCE). Three major dynasties emerged, named after their respective founders, the Ptolemaic (after Ptolemy I), which controlled Egypt, Cyprus, the southern Levant including Judaea, and part of the eastern Aegean, the Antipatrid (after Antipater I *Monophthalmos*), in

14   ANTIOCH AND JERUSALEM

Macedonia and the Seleucid (after Seleucus I). Seleucus gained the largest and well-endowed portion, extending from Asia Minor in the west to the Indian frontier in the east, and including Syria, Mesopotamia and Persia. He established two capitals from which to administer his enormous kingdom, Antioch-on-the-Orontes in the west and Seleucia-on-the-Tigris in the east.

Ptolemy 1 was the most successful of the *Diadochi*, creating an empire that spanned the eastern end of the Mediterranean, and living to the ripe age of 84. Note the tiny Greek letter Δ behind the ear of the portrait, which is believed to represent the 'signature' of the Hellenistic artist or die engraver.

The ruling élite of the "successor" states was Greek-speaking, each one led by a monarchy of Macedonian descent. Each adopted an era based on the year of its foundation, which for the Seleucid kingdom was 312/311 BCE (counted as year 1 of the Seleucid Era; abbreviated as SE 1).

Citing a report by the by 2nd century BCE Greek historian Agatharchides of Cnidus (now lost), Josephus notes that Ptolemy I captured Jerusalem on a Sabbath without any resistance, because its Jewish inhabitants refused to bear arms that day and also they fell for the ruse that Ptolemy had arrived to make a sacrifice in the Temple [Josephus, *AJ* 12.4-6].

Once in control, the Ptolemies exerted fairly tight economic grip over Judah (as it did over its other possessions), including the levying of taxes, as ascertained from surviving papyri. A particularly important source of information is the cache of Zenon papyri, which cover the years 261 to the 240s BCE. Zenon was a procurement agent and supervisor for Ptolemy II and Ptolemy III, whose archives were fortuitously preserved and rediscovered in the 20th

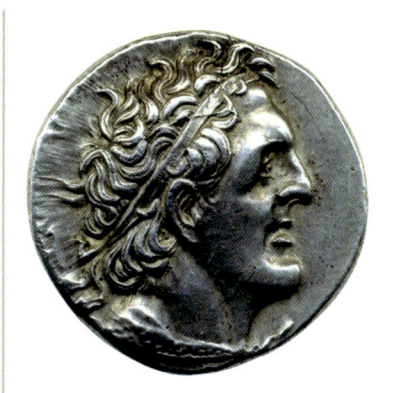

Ill. 2.3. Ptolemy I Soter (323-282 BCE). AR tetradrachm (27 mm, 14.91 gm), struck c. 298-285 BCE. Alexandria mint. Diademed head of Ptolemy I / Eagle standing on a thunderbolt, Φ and monogram to the left. The Greek inscription reads ΒΑΣΙΛΕΩΣ ΠΤΟΛΕΜΑΙΟΥ, "of King Ptolemy". Svoronos no. 267.

Ill. 2.4. Seleucus I Nicator (ruled as king 305/4-281 BCE). AR tetradrachm (28 mm, 17.17 gm). Tarsus mint, 282- 281 BCE. Head of Herakles in a lion's skin headdress / Zeus seated on throne, holding a Nike offering a wreath in his right hand and a sceptre in his left; monograms in the left field and beneath the throne. The Greek inscription reads ΒΑΣΙΛΕΩΣ ΣΕΛΕΥΚΟΥ, "of King Seleucus". *SC* no. 10.1.

This piece is based on a coin type of Alexander the Great, but with the Nike (the winged personification of victory) replacing an eagle on the Alexander issues, possibly connected with Seleucus' contest with Lysimachus of Thrace that resulted in his victory at Corupedium in 281 BCE and conquest of Asia Minor.

century at Philadelphia in the Fayum, Egypt, where he went into retirement. Zenon travelled through the southern Levant for the better part of a year between 259 and 258 BCE as the commercial agent of Apollonius, the Egyptian minister of finance (*dioketes*), looking after his interests, including estates, and undertaking various transactions on his behalf in the places visited.

Matters of religion and also, to a large extent, the day-to-day management of affairs in Judaea were left to the High Priest of Jerusalem, probably assisted by a council of notables, which eventually evolved into the Sanhedrin. The Ptolemies generally respected and did not interfere in the beliefs of their subjects, the majority of whom, in Egypt, were faithful to their ancestral cults. During the period of Ptolemaic suzerainty, tiny silver coins, which had been issued fairly steadily by Judah from about the mid-4th century BCE (under its Aramaic name, Yehud), continued to be produced. Common types are of similar design to the Ptolemaic tetradrachms, bearing the head of the monarch on their obverse (or left blank) and an eagle on their reverse, but in miniature. Apparently, Judaea was virtually unique among the Ptolemaic possessions in the Levant in being permitted to issue silver fractional coins in its own name and inscribed in its regional palaeo-Hebrew script. However, its minting rights seem to have been withdrawn when regular precious-metal production ceased at all other Syro-Phoenician mints in the 6th year of Ptolemy III, in 141/0 BCE: Ake-Ptolemais (Acre), Iopé/Joppa (Jaffa) and Gaza had briefly exercised minting rights from 261/0 BCE.

The imitation of Ptolemaic motifs on coins of Judaea is a manifestation of the infiltration of Greek culture into Jewish society but it is by no means the earliest instance. Athenian coins and pottery dating back to the 5th century have been found frequently throughout the southern Levant, including Judah, while it still belonged to the Persian Empire. In about 400 BCE, or a few decades into the 4th century BCE, Yehud began to issue small silver coins based on the Attic weight system and modelled on Athenian silver currency, featuring the profiled head of Athena on the obverse and well-known owl motif on the reverse [*TJC*, 6-8, 10, nos. 2-12]. Greek influences certainly deepened after the advent of Macedonian rule in the Levant, particularly through the strengthening of trade ties with the Aegean and other parts of the Greek world. On the one hand, they enriched the economic and cultural life of Judaea, as Judah was known in the classical period, but the encounter between Judaea and the Greek world also generated tension, erupting into bitter conflict in the mid-2nd century BCE, with the wars of the Maccabees.

In the neighbouring Seleucid kingdom, Seleucus I Nicator (305/4-281 BCE) was followed by Antiochus I Soter (281–261 BCE), Antiochus II Theos (261-246 BCE), Seleucus II Callinicus (246-226 BCE) and Seleucus III Ceraunus (226-223 BCE). All these rulers found it difficult to assert their authority over their unwieldy territories, with their plethora of nationalities, languages and religions, and they frequently had to deal

Ill. 2.5. Judaea, under Ptolemy I (or Ptolemy II). AR quarter obol (or tetartemorion; 7 mm, 0.22 gm and 6 mm, 0.18 gm, respectively), struck c. 295/294 - c. 283 BCE (or c. 283/2- after 270 BCE). Jerusalem mint. (a) Blank obverse / Eagle perched on a thunderbolt. The Aramaic inscription reads YHD, "Judah". This coin belongs to type **http://menorahcoinproject.org/yhd-34.htm**, blank/R5, the reverse being similar to Gitler and Lorber 2006, Group 5, no. 7, which bears a profiled and diademed portrait of Ptolemy I on the obverse, as in example (b), of type **http://menorahcoinproject.org/yhd-36.htm**, O3/R18: note the thunderbolt beneath the feet of the eagle, which is clearly visible on the reverse of this example.

a – left,
b – right

THE LEGACY OF ALEXANDER THE GREAT

Ill. 2.6. Antiochos I (281-261 BCE), Æ dichalkon (18 mm, 6.0 gm). Antioch mint. Macedonian shield (alluding to the homeland of Seleucus with his dynastic emblem, the inverted anchor, in central boss) / Elephant walking; monogram and club above, jawbone in exergue. The Greek inscription reads ΒΑΣΙΛΕΩΣ ΑΝΤΙΟΧΟΥ, "of King Antiochus". *SC* no. 339.3.

with rebellions, secessions, bitter conflict with rival Hellenistic kingdoms and, in the case of Seleucus II, a damaging civil war with his brother, Antiochus Hierax. Not long after the commencement of the reign of Antiochus I, in 268 BCE, Anatolia was invaded by three Galatian tribes, which formed part of the great Celtic migration across Eurasia. Three years later, Antiochus inflicted a major defeat on the Gauls using his detachment of Indian war elephants. In recognition of his victory, Antiochus I acquired the epithet *Soter* (Greek for "saviour").

The traditional explanation of the association of the anchor with the Seleucids is that Seleucus I was fathered by the god Apollo and that the deity gave a ring set with a stone engraved with an anchor to the king's mother, Laodice, as a gift for her sexual favours. Also, it was claimed that Seleucus was born with a birthmark shaped like an anchor and this 'blemish' was inherited by his sons and grandsons (Justin, *Epitome* 15.4.3-6; Appian, *Syriaca* 56). However, it is rather more likely that this symbol was originally adopted by Seleucus as a mark of his distinction as admiral of the fleet of Ptolemy I in 315/4 BCE [Diodorus Siculus 19.58.5-6; 19.60.3-4;19.62.4]. The Indian elephant on this coin publicises a formidable military asset of the Seleucids, the horns being added to this image of the beast to symbolise divinely-endowed strength. Consignments of elephants were received periodically as tribute from rulers of Bactria and India

CHAPTER 3

ANTIOCHUS III AND SELEUCUS IV - THE PRELUDE TO THE MACCABAEAN REBELLION

Antiochus III *Megas*, (223–187 BCE) [Grainger 1997, 15-22; *SC* 1.1, 351-54], younger son of Seleucus II Callinicus (246-226 BCE), became the 6th ruler of the Seleucid Empire as a youth of about eighteen, following the assassination of his elder brother Seleucus III Ceraunus (226-223 BCE).

Antiochus III inherited a kingdom in disarray: the easternmost provinces had broken away during the reign of his father, Bactria under Diodotus II, and Parthia under the nomad chieftain Arsaces. Soon after Antiochus' accession, Babylonia and Persis (Persia) revolted under their governors Molon and his brother Alexander. Generals sent against the two rebel governors by Antiochus' chief minister, Hermias (inherited from his father), met with failure. Antiochus next responded by leading an army himself, which prevailed, resulting in Molon and Alexander committing suicide (in 220 BCE). Antiochus then advanced into Media Atropatene (modern Azerbaijan), which had joined the revolt. After snuffing out this rebellion, Antiochus returned to Antioch, the Seleucid capital, and executed the ineffectual Hermias.

These coin portraits on Antioch issues provide a fairly consistent representation of Antiochus III from the early to middle years of his reign. Apollo had been

Ill. 3.1. Antiochus III Megas (223-187 BCE). AR tetradrachms (31 mm, 17.01 gm and 29 mm, 17.02 gm, respectively). Antioch mint. Diademed head of Antiochus III / Apollo seated on the *omphalos* ("navel") of Delphi, symbolising the centre of the world. He examines an arrow in his right hand and holds a bow in his left; monogram in the outer left field. The Greek inscription reads ΒΑΣΙΛΕΩΣ ΑΝΤΙΟΧΟΥ, "of King Antiochus". (a) ***Above***: 204-199 BCE, *SC* no. 1044.4a. (b) ***Below***: 195-187 BCE, *SC* no. 1045.6.

Ill. 3.2. Achaeus (usurper, 220-214 BCE). Æ dichalkon (16 mm, 5.69 gm). Sardes mint. Laureate head of Apollo / Eagle standing with palm branch behind. The Greek inscription reads ΒΑΣΙΛΕΩ[Σ] ΑΧΑΙΟ[Υ], "of King Achaeus". *SC* no. 955.

established as the patron deity of the Seleucid dynasty by its founder, Seleucus Nicator, who had built an impressive shrine to this god at Daphne, near Antioch. He and his successors also patronised the famous temple of Apollo at Didyma near Miletus in Ionia.

That same year, a revolt broke out in Asia Minor, involving Achaeus, who was a kinsman of the Seleucid royal house and had hitherto been an important supporter of Antiochus. Achaeus proclaimed himself king in Asia Minor, but his mercenary army refused to march on Antioch, giving Antiochus valuable time to prepare a campaign against him. His army made its move in 216 BCE, taking all the territory that had been held by Achaeus. The usurper was cornered in his last stronghold, the citadel of Sardis, where he was captured and impaled in c. 214 BCE.

Meanwhile, Antiochus chalked up another important success, recovering Seleucia Pieria from Ptolemaic control in 219 BCE. This city was of dynastic interest, as it housed the tomb of the founder of the dynasty and city, Seleucus Nicator, but was also strategically important, serving as the major port of the capital, Antioch, situated higher up the River Orontes. Its conquest by Ptolemy III Euergetes in 246 BCE had temporarily deprived the Seleucid capital of its use. Antiochus wasted little time and launched an offensive against Ptolemaic possessions in the southern Levant, making rapid gains until meeting defeat at Raphia by the forces of Ptolemy IV Philopator at the southern border of Palestine in 217 BCE, which forced him to give up all his gains apart from Seleucia Pieria. Next, Antiochus turned north, extending Seleucid control over Armenia (212-211 BCE). In 209 BCE he struck east, receiving the submission of the Parthians and then launched an attack on Bactria. Heavy fighting with the Bactrian king, Euthydemus, kept Antiochus occupied from 208 to 206 BCE, but it ended with Euthydemus submitting to Seleucid rule and surrendering his war elephants. Following the footsteps of Alexander the Great, Antiochus proceeded into Mauryan India, where he cemented an accord with its king, Sophagesenus, who presented him with a further gift of elephants. Again, following Alexander's rout, Antiochus returned westward along the coast to Mesopotamia, encountering resistance from the Arabs of Gerrha on the Persian Gulf (205/4 BCE), but ending in a peace treaty. Antiochus celebrated the 20th anniversary of his rule and successful completion of his *anabasis* in Babylon in the Spring of 204 BCE.

In 204 BCE the infant Ptolemy V Epiphanes succeeded to the Egyptian throne and Antiochus is said (notably by Polybius) to have concluded a secret pact with Philip V of Macedon to carve up the Ptolemaic overseas possessions between them in 203 BCE. Once again, Antiochus invaded and occupied the entire Levant, i.e., Coele-Syria (or Koile Syria) and Phoenicia, including Judaea, in 202 BCE. The region was briefly recovered by Ptolemy V, but then Antiochus scored a resounding victory over Ptolemy's forces, commanded by his commander-in-chief, Scopas, at Panion (in 200 BCE), which resulted in the annexation of the entire southern Levant to the Seleucid kingdom by 198 BCE. Antiochus was conciliatory towards his new subjects, including the Jews, and also confirmed the administrative autonomy of Judaea under his rule. According to Josephus,

Ill. 3.3. Ptolemy V Epiphanes (204-180 BCE). AR tetradrachm (27 mm, 13.94 gm). Tyre mint. c. 202-200 BCE. Diademed and draped bust of Ptolemy V / Eagle standing on a thunderbolt; to the left, a club surmounted by the Tyre monogram, NI to the right and ΔI between the legs. The Greek inscription reads ΒΑΣΙΛΕΩΣ ΠΤΟΛΕΜΑΙΟΥ, "of King Ptolemy". Mørkholm *Portraits*, pl. 23, 12; Svoronos no. 1297. Spink Auction 3014 (8 October 2003), lot 109; courtesy of Spink & Son.

Ill. 3.4. Antiochus III Megas. Æ tetrachalkon (23 mm. 7.44 gm). Tyre mint. Struck in year SE 116 (PIC) = 197/6 BCE. Obverse: Diademed head of Antiochus III / Stern of galley. The Greek inscription reads ΒΑΣΙΛΕΩΣ ΑΝΤΙΟΧΟΥ, "of King Antiochus", together with the date. *SC* no. 1078.3.

The Phoenician war galley is discussed in the captions to Ills. 5.10 and 5.11.

the Jews opened the gates of Jerusalem to Antiochus and his troops and supplied them with provisions. They also assisted Antiochus' men in gaining the surrender of the city's citadel and garrison left there by Scopas. In appreciation of the friendly reception that he received in Jerusalem, Antiochus issued a decree addressed to Ptolemy, the Seleucid governor of Coele-Syria, confirming his grant of rights and privileges to the civil administration and citizens of Jerusalem. Among these was a gift of provisions for the Temple, a three-year exemption from taxes and assistance to inhabitants who had left the city during the conflict and wished to return. He also issued an edict in support of maintaining the ritual purity of Jerusalem and the Temple [Josephus, *AJ* 12.133-146]. However, there was to be no resumption of autonomous Judaean coinage, and the Jerusalem mint would only reopen for business 70 years later, during the reign of Antiochus VII *Sidetes*.

With a string of stunning victories behind him and in possession of a much expanded kingdom, extending from the Sinai peninsula to the Indus River, Antiochus began to style himself "Great King" (*Basileus Megas*), no doubt in emulation of the Persian Achaeminids, whose empire Antiochus had effectively rebuilt [Ma 1999, Appendix 4, 272-76].

In his next campaign (in 197 BCE), Antiochus endeavoured to take control the coastal towns of Asia Minor, which were in the Ptolemaic orbit. He met with success in Asia Minor and a peace was reached with Egypt, ending the Fifth Syrian War, and celebrated by a union between Antiochus' daughter, Cleopatra, and Ptolemy V at Raphia in the winter of 193/2 BCE. Thereafter, Cleopatra was adopted as a frequent name for Ptolemaic princesses.

During Antiochus' Ionian campaign, he twice crossed over into Europe, penetrating Thrace (195 and 194 BCE), taking advantage of the defeat of Philip V by the Romans at Cynoscephalae in 197 BCE. His expansionist agenda, particularly in the West, came to a head when he invaded Greece with a large army at the invitation of the Aetolian League (a confederation of states in central Greece) and egged on by Hannibal, now a fugitive with Antiochus. This brought Antiochus into direct conflict with Rome, with Greek cities and states in Asia Minor, notably Pergamon, appealing to Rome for help.

Rome declared war on Antiochus and sent a force under Manius Acilius Glabrio, which routed Antiochus' army at Thermopylae (where three centuries earlier, the Greeks has won a crucial victory over the Persians) and obliged him to withdraw to Asia (in 191 BCE). The Romans followed up their success by advancing into Anatolia. Antiochus' crushing defeat at the hands of Scipio Asiaticus at Magnesia on Mt. Sipylus (in 190/189 BCE), following the defeat of Hannibal at sea off Side, delivered Asia Minor into Roman hands.

By the Treaty of Apamea (188 BCE) the Seleucid king was forced to surrender all land north and west of the Taurus, which Rome distributed amongst its allies. The terms under this treaty were harsh. Antiochus had to relinquish his war elephants and Seleucid naval use of the Aegean was greatly restricted. In addition, Antiochus was obliged to pay an indemnity of 15,000 silver talents, to be paid in twelve annual instalments. As a consequence of this enormous blow to Seleucid power, outlying provinces of the empire, which had been recovered by Antiochus, reasserted their independence. Antiochus mounted a fresh expedition to the east, where he died at the hands of an angry mob while attempting to rob a temple of Bel/Zeus at Elymaïs, Persia, in 187 BCE, probably to collect bullion towards the war indemnity. The Seleucid kingdom then fell to his son, Seleucus.

Principal Ancient Sources:
Appian, *Syriaca* 1; 5; 12-20; 30-36.
Cassius Dio, 19.
Diodorus Siculus, 28.3; 29.15; 31.19.
Eusebius, *Chronicon* 1.40.12.
Josephus, *Antiquitates Judaicae* (*AJ*) 12.129-155.
Justin, *Epitome* 30.2.
Livy, *Ab urbe condita* 31.14; 32.8; 33.19-20, 31, 34, 38-42, 44-45, 49; 34.33, 57-61; 35.12-34, 42-51; 36.1-22, 41-44; 37.8, 18-56; 38.37-38.
Livy, *Periochae* 33.8; 34.10; 35.10; 36.1; 37.1-5, 7-10; 38.9; 39.7; 41.5.
Plutarch, *Moralia* (*Regum et Imperatorum apophthegmata*) 183F.
Polybius, 2.71; 4.48, 51; 5.40-87; 8.15-23; 9.43; 10.27-31; 11.34, 39; 13.9; 15.20; 16.18-20, 39; 20.8; 21.6-24, 42.
Strabo, *Geographia* 16.1.18.

(a)

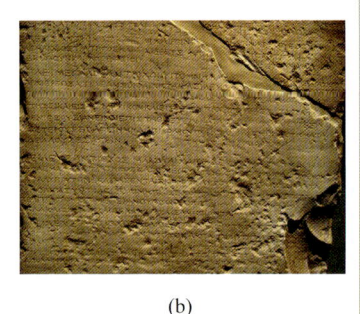

(b)

Ill. 3.5 (a, b) Hefzibah Stele found in the Scythopolis Plain (the south-eastern end of the Jezreel Valley). Courtesy of the Israel Museum, Jerusalem.

THE HEFZIBAH STELE

The Hefzibah Stele inscription dates from 201-195 BCE, i.e. immediately after Antiochus III's conquest of the southern Levant. It reproduces five letters exchanged between the king and Ptolemy son of Thraseas, governor (*strategos*) and high priest (*archiereus*) of Syria-Phoenicia, who has been awarded land in the plain of Scythopolis (Beth-shean). He appears to have been a military commander in the Ptolemaic army who was granted the land as a reward for his defection. The letters refer to the governor's ownership of villages in the plain and indicate that the same official's heirs were entitled to inherit them. In this correspondence, Ptolemy asks Antiochus III to forbid his soldiers from requisitioning billets in local homes and forcing inhabitants into service. He declares his support to this petition, ordering his subordinates to desist from this practice and stipulating punishment for all transgressors. See Landau 1966; Bertrand 1982.

Seleucus IV Philopator [Grainger 1997, 63-65; *SC* 2.1, 1-2], ruled from 187 BCE to 175 BCE over a realm consisting of Syria (which included Cilicia, Phoenicia and Palestine), Mesopotamia, Babylonia and southern Iran (Media and Persia).

The eldest son of Antiochus III, Antiochus predeceased his father, leaving his second son, Seleucus, as heir to the Seleucid kingdom, which he inherited in 187 BCE. As a prince of the realm, he had supported his father's invasion of Greece, although remaining in Asia Minor, laying siege to Pergamon, Rome's ally. Seleucus participated in the battle of Magnesia with Antiochus III and shared in his defeat.

There is evidence from inscriptions that Seleucus IV bore the epithet "Philopator

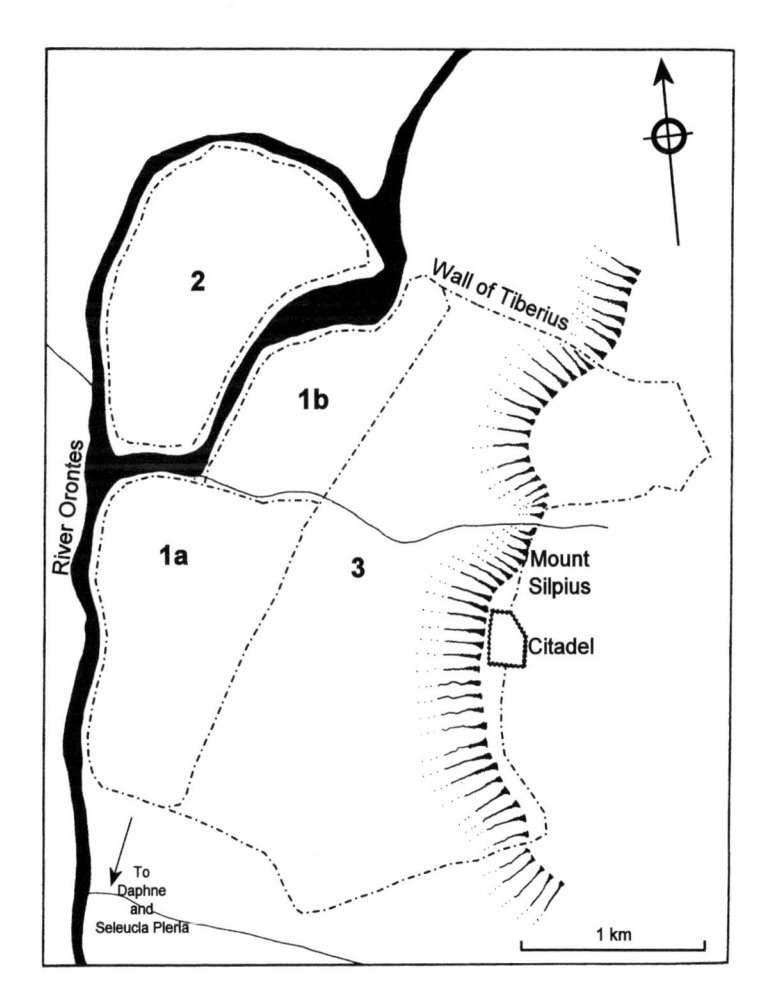

Ill. 3.6. Antioch was founded by Seleucus Nicator on the River Orontes (1a), at the junction between Anatolia and Syria. Its citadel was established on Mt. Silpius overlooking the city from the east, with and the city occupied the low ground between the mountain and the river. It was laid out on a grid plan by the Greek architect Xenarius, with its two main thoroughfares intersecting in the centre. Antiochus I extended the city eastwards (1b) and Seleucus II Callinicus initiated a third new quarter on an adjoining island in the Orontes, which was completed by his son Antiochus III (2). A fourth quarter (3) was added by Antiochus IV Epiphanes. Its population was drawn from a mix of local inhabitants, Greeks and other communities drawn from further afield, including Jews. It was made the western capital of the Seleucid realm by Antiochus I (the eastern capital being Seleucia-on-the-Tigris). By the late Hellenistic period Antioch's population reached its peak of about half a million inhabitants and it became the third largest city in the Roman Empire after Rome and Alexandria.

Ill. 3.7. Seleucus IV Philopator (187-175 BCE). AR tetradrachms (28 mm, 17.04 and 30 mm, 16.76 gm respectively), struck c. 180-175 BCE. Diademed head of Seleucus IV / Apollo seated on an omphalos, holding arrow in right hand, his left hand resting on a bow. The Greek inscription reads ΒΑΣΙΛΕΩΣ ΣΕΛΕΥΚΟΥ, "of King Seleucus". (a) *Above*: Antioch mint. On the reverse, Filleted palm to the outer left, Φ monogram in exergue. *SC* no. 1313.6b. (b) *Below*: Ake-Ptolemais mint. On the reverse, AB monogram to the inner left and IA in exergue. *SC* no. 1331a. These are coin portraits of Seleucus from the Seleucid metropolis and a provincial mint in the southern Levant, respectively.

(father-loving)", which is fitting for the son of such a celebrated father, although this title does not appear on his coins, in accordance with the practice of his forebears.

This coin highlights the prominence accorded to the cult of Apollo by the Seleucids until the reign of Antiochus IV.

Perhaps this chastening military experience was responsible for Seleucus abjuring his father's expansionist policy, but instead concentrated on buttressing the security of his kingdom and building a defensive alliance against Rome, notably with Macedonia, giving his daughter Laodice in marriage to Perseus, its last king. Although his freedom of action would have been heavily restricted by the Treaty of Apamea, he seems to have ignored some of its provisions, including forgoing war elephants and limiting the size of his fleet. Seleucus also seems to have failed to keep up the annual indemnity payment to Rome. In about 178 BCE, his brother, Mithradates (the future Antiochus IV) was replaced as surety in Rome by Seleucus' oldest son, Demetrius.

In 175 BCE, Seleucus was murdered by his chancellor, Heliodorus, who attempted to seize the Syrian crown, declaring the victim's younger son, Antiochus, then a child no more than five years old, as titular king, with his mother Laodice as regent.

For much of the reign of Seleucus IV, Jerusalem continued to enjoy peace and prosperity. The serving High Priest and Jewish leader, Onias (Honiah), was held in esteem for his piety and integrity. We are told that the Temple in Jerusalem was honoured by Seleucus, who subsidised its sacrifices out of his royal purse.

This tranquillity was shattered by a quarrel between the Temple administrator, Simon of the Bilgah priestly clan, and Onias about the regulation of the city market. Unable to prevail over Onias, Simon turned to Apollonius, the Seleucid governor of Coele-Syria and Phoenicia, and mischievously disclosed that the Temple treasury in Jerusalem was full of riches, there for the taking. The king sent his chief minister, Heliodorus, to Jerusalem to seize this treasure. The High Priest resisted him, pleading that the money in the treasury was set aside for widows and orphans; but Heliodorus paid no heed and entered the Temple. There, in response to the prayers of the High Priest, it is reputed that he was stopped short by the apparition of a rider in golden armour on a finely caparisoned horse bearing down on him, while two Adonises of strong physique scourged him mercilessly. Heliodorus was rendered insensible and carried out of the Temple in a stupor. Only by a special sacrifice offered by the High Priest was he restored to consciousness. Heliodorus, grateful for his recovery, left the Temple untouched, and returned to Seleucus with an account of his experience. Questioned by him as to whom he should next send to Jerusalem for the treasure, Heliodorus advised him to send his worst enemy, for he would return soundly flogged, if at

Ill. 3.8. Seleucus IV Philopator. Æ tetrachalkon (21 mm, 10.14 gm). Antioch mint. Wreathed head of Apollo / Apollo Delphius standing, leaning on a tripod and holding an arrow. The Greek inscription reads ΒΑΣΙΛΕΩΣ ΣΕΛΕΥΚΟΥ, "of King Seleucus". *SC* no. 1315.7e.

all. The bitter hostility of Simon towards Onias festered and we encounter his notorious brother, Menelaus, wreaking havoc in Jerusalem during the reign of Antiochus IV Epiphanes [2 Macc. 3.1-4.6].

Ill. 3.9. The Expulsion of Heliodorus, Chief Minister of Seleucus IV, from the Temple (2 Macc. 3.22-30). Fresco painting by Raphael in the Stanza di Eliodoro, Vatican Palace, dating from 1511-12

Principal Ancient Sources:
2 Maccabees 3-4.6.
Appian, *Syriaca* 26; 33; 39; 45; 66.
Diodorus Siculus 29.17, 24.
Eusebius, *Chronicon* p. 253.
Justin, *Epitome* 34.3-8.
Livy, *Ab urbe condita* 33.40; 35.15; 37.11, 18, 21; 38.13; 42.12.
Livy, *Periochae* 46.12.
Polybius, 18.51; 21.6; 22.7; 25.4.

THE HELIODORUS STELE

A recently deciphered stele from the Hellenistic settlement at Marisa (biblical Maresha; see below), south-west of Jerusalem, on display at the Israel Museum, presents new information about Heliodorus [Cotton, and M. Wörrle 2007; Gera 2009]. The stele bears an edict from Seleucus IV, dated to the summer of 178 BCE, in the form of a letter to his chief minister (literally, "who is in charge of the affairs"), Heliodorus, about the appointment of a certain Olympiodorus to supervise the cults in Coele-Syria and Phoenicia (i.e. the southern Levant). Olympiodorus is described as a chamberlain of the king and a member of his inner circle (belonging to the rank of "First Friends").

The royal edict is prefaced by two shorter letters, one from Dorymenes, the Governor (*strategos*) of Coele-Syria and Phoenicia, to Diophanes, the official responsible for Marisa and its district, and the other from Heliodorus to Dorymenes. The gist of this preamble is to confirm the transmission of the edict through the chain of command from the king down to the local level.

In his edict, Seleucus IV expresses his duty of care for the security and well-being of his subjects. He is aware that the achievement of a happy state of affairs ("good fortune") requires "the favour of the gods", which can only happen if "the established sanctuaries" of the realm are provided with "the proper service".

For all these soothing words, Olympiodorus' tasks were to police and also to raise money from the various sanctuaries of Coele-Syria and Phoenicia. In 2 Maccabees' account of the attempt to despoil the Temple of Jerusalem, it seems that Olympiodorus was replaced by the more senior and sinister figure of Heliodorus to heighten the significance of this episode. Such interference in the affairs of the Jewish Temple must have riled the priestly authorities in Jerusalem and served as a foretaste of Antiochus IV's wholesale appropriation of their Temple and its contents.

First, the large upper portion of this stele appeared on the antiquities market. Later, three other inscribed fragments were found amid spoil in a cave at Marisa, increasing the number of lines of recovered text to 36. These fragments have now been reunited with the main portion of the stele, as shown in the photograph.

Ill. 3.10. Heliodorus Stele from Marisa. Courtesy of the Israel Museum, Jerusalem

CHAPTER 4.

ANTIOCHUS IV AND THE OUTBREAK OF THE REBELLION

Antiochus IV Theos Epiphanes (175–164 BCE) [Grainger 1997, 22-27; *SC* 2.1, 41-44], was in his late thirties and residing in Athens when his brother Seleucus was assassinated. Seeing his chance, Antiochus made a bid for the Seleucid throne. Arriving in Asia Minor, he was met by Eumenes of Pergamon, welcomed as king, and escorted by a Pergamene army to the frontier of the Seleucid kingdom. He proclaimed himself co-regent with Seleucus' young child, Antiochus, who he adopted. He seems to have married Seleucus' widow, because his wife's name was also Laodice. No doubt, such a step would have helped to legitimise Antiochus' assumption of power. Following the birth of his first son, the future Antiochus V, he orchestrated the murder of his nephew (and stepson), who he now regarded as an impediment. With Antiochus on the throne, we hear no more about Heliodorus, who either fled the Seleucid kingdom or was executed.

The choice of Zeus on the reverse Antiochus' tetradrachms in place of Apollo reflects his promotion of the cult of the chief Olympian deity. This subject had been last used on Seleucid coins more than a century earlier (see Ill. 2.4). Antiochus' adoption of "god manifest" as a formal title from about 173/2 BCE was a signal to his subjects to revere him as a divine being. The epithet "victorious" was added following his Egyptian campaign in 170 BCE.

Antiochus IV is described by Polybius [28.18] as an able and energetic ruler.

Ill. 4.1. Antiochus IV Theos Epiphanes (175-164 BCE). AR tetradrachm (30 mm, 16.89 gm), struck c. 168-164 BCE. Antioch mint. Diademed head of Antiochus IV / Zeus seated, holding a Nike with a wreath in his right hand and sceptre in his left; monogram in the outer left field. The Greek inscription reads ΒΑΣΙΛΕΩΣ ΑΝΤΙΟΧΟΥ ΘΕΟΥ ΕΠΙΦΑΝΟΥΣ ΝΙΚΗΦΟΡΟΥ, "of King Antiochus, *Theou Epiphanous Nikephorou* ("god manifest, the victorious"). *SC* no. 1400d.

According to Livy [*Ab urbe condita* 42.6.7], early in his reign Antiochus IV managed to pay off the indemnity to Rome, although his rapacious actions would suggest otherwise. His seizure of the throne from his brother's heirs would plunge the Seleucid house in dynastic strife for generations. Antiochus' own reign, which began on a high note, was destined to end in disappointment and failure. Towards the end of 170 BCE, the young king of Egypt, Ptolemy VI Philometor, made a rash attempt to regain the southern Levant. This aggression gave Antiochus the pretext to strike back and his army resoundingly defeated the Ptolemaic forces, enabling Antiochus to enter Egypt and establish a base in Memphis, where he received Ptolemy VI. A new rival king, Ptolemy VIII Euergetes was proclaimed at Alexandria and the Ptolemaic capital had to endure a siege by Antiochus. Antiochus was forced to cut short his expedition and return to Syria in the autumn of 169 BCE.

In the spring of 168 BCE, Antiochus again invaded Egypt while his fleet captured Cyprus, which had been a Ptolemaic possession. Outside Alexandria he was met by Gaius Popillius Laenas, an envoy of the Roman Republic, who ordered him to immediately withdraw from Egypt and Cyprus. Antiochus said he would discuss this demand with his council, whereupon Laenas drew round him a line in the sand, and said: "Before you cross this circle I want you to give me a reply for the Roman senate". The implication was that, were he to step out of the circle without an immediate commitment to withdraw from Egypt, the Seleucid king would find himself at war with Rome. Appreciating his predicament, Antiochus promised to withdraw and only then Laenas agreed to shake hands with him. It was the year of the Roman victory over Perseus of Macedon at Pydna, where his kingdom met its end and, as Polybius [29.27.12-13] points out, if it had not been for that resounding Roman triumph on 22 June 168 BCE, Antiochus IV might not have been so ready to accede to Laenas' ultimatum.

The momentous encounter between Antiochus and the Roman envoy outside Alexandria is also recorded in the biblical Book of Daniel [11.30]: ובאו בו ציים כתים ונכאה ("and ships of the *Kittim* [a western people, i.e. Romans] will come against him [Antiochus] and he will be rebuffed") as a prophecy rather than a contemporary event – which it was.

As a result of the intervention of Laenas, Antiochus was obliged to evacuate his forces from Cyprus, besides having to abort his offensive against Egypt. Rome was now the unchallenged master of the eastern Mediterranean, a position that it held until the Arab invasions of the 7th century CE.

Besides his two abortive campaigns in Egypt, Antiochus made the mistake of interfering with the administration and finances of indigenous sanctuaries, including the Temple in Jerusalem and the great Esagila temple of Marduk in Babylon [Geller 1991, 1-4]. In the case of Jerusalem, we possess a detailed account. The king had broken his father's pledge to the Jews to respect their religious autonomy by meddling in the appointment of High Priest after the death of Onias (Honiah) III, eventually choosing the unscrupulous and destructive Menelaus. On his way back to Antioch from his first Egyptian campaign, Antiochus stopped off in Jerusalem and pillaged the city, but on his second visit there, in 268/7 BCE, he encountered resolute opposition and proceeded to plunder the Temple and massacre the inhabitants. His cruel acts precipitated the Maccabaean uprising.

In 166 BCE, Antiochus staged a month long festival at Daphne, 9 km south of Antioch, in which he flaunted his opulence and military power to which he invited guests from across the Greek world. There, as at Athens (see below), he represented himself as a leading exponent of Hellenic religion and culture. He was also responsible for founding or refounding several new cities in his kingdom, an act that earned a Hellenistic ruler considerable prestige.

Antiochus' last years were spent on campaign against the ascendant Parthians, led by Phraates I (168-165 BCE), who had occupied Seleucid Hyrcania. His expedition seems to have been successful initially, beating the Armenians into submission and capturing their capital, Artaxias. He then proceeded further east to Elymais, where he is said to have attempted to extract money from a temple of Nanaia in Elymais, but was repelled by the natives. Soon afterwards, he fell ill and died in the autumn of 164 at Tabae (an unidentified place not far from modern Isphahan). The reign of Antiochus was the last period of glory for the Seleucid kingdom and it sowed the seeds for a rapid decline: he was a usurper, with dangerous internal foes, and he left the Seleucid throne in the hands of a vulnerable child, his son, Antiochus V Eupator.

Ill. 4.2. Antiochus IV Theos Epiphanes. Æ dichalkon (17 mm, 3.64 gm). Ake-Ptolemais mint, c. 175-173/2 BCE. Veiled female bust, representing Demeter, or Laodice IV [see Huth, Potts and Hoover, 2002] or the latter as Demeter; monogram behind / Elephant head; monogram in front and the prow of a warship behind. The Greek inscription reads ΒΑΣΙΛΕΩΣ ΑΝΤΙΟΧΟΥ, "of King Antiochus". *SC* no. 1477.2b.

Laodice IV was the widow of Antiochus' brother, Seleucus IV. Indian elephants constituted the heavy armour divisions of Seleucid armies and, only a decade after the date of this coin, one of the Maccabee brothers, Eleazar, died attacking a war elephant, which he believed bore the ruling king, Antiochus V, during the hard-fought battle of Beth-zechariah. The war galley refers to Ake-Ptolemais as a major port and a base of the Seleucid fleet.

Shortly after Antiochus IV succeeded to the Seleucid throne, Jason (Yeshua), Onias' brother usurped the high-priesthood, offering the king, who was a fervent advocate of Greek religion and culture, an enormous bribe, with even more if the king allowed him to convert Jerusalem into a Greek-style civic community (a *polis*) dedicated to Antiochus. Jason also undertook to establish there a gymnasium and a *ephebium* to initiate the youth of the city into a Greek way of life. This was an offer that Antiochus could not refuse. Jason's commitment to Antiochus and his Greek values was unstinting and we are told that he sent representatives from Jerusalem to the quinquennial games at Tyre, attended by the king, bearing 300 drachms intended to pay for a sacrifice to Hercules, but diverted to equipping Antiochus' war fleet. Jason personally welcomed him to Jerusalem "with torchlight and ovations" [2 Macc. 4.7-22; in this account reference will mostly be made to the primary sources, 1 Maccabees (heavily relied on by Josephus) and 2 Maccabees].

Three years later, Jason sent Menelaus, the brother of the Simon who had instigated the attempted plunder of the Temple treasury by Heliodorus, on a mission to Antiochus. He used the opportunity to outbid Jason for the high priesthood in Jerusalem, and gained a royal warrant for this position. Jason was obliged to leave Jerusalem and seek refuge across the Jordan. At the same time, Onias sought sanctuary at the famous Seleucid temple to Apollo in Daphne, 9 km south of Antioch. Menelaus schemed to have Onias lured from the precincts of Apollo and murdered [2 Macc 4.23-34].

Menelaus and another brother, Lysimachus, plundered and sold off gold vessels from the Temple, much to the fury of the inhabitants of Jerusalem. On a false report that Antiochus had died during an invasion of Egypt, Jason made an abortive bid to recapture the city, involving many civilian casualties. Jason ended his life as a fugitive. To add to all this misery, on his way back from a failed expedition to Egypt in 169 or 168 BCE, Antiochus sacked Jerusalem and pillaged and desecrated the Temple, with the connivance of Menelaus. Officials that he left behind continued to perpetrate outrages on the population and the Temple. Moreover, to reinforce Seleucid control over Jerusalem and its inhabitants, a sturdy citadel (the *Akra*) was erected in a strategic position overlooking the Temple [2 Macc. 4.39-5.26; 1 Macc. 1.20-40].

In 167 BCE, Antiochus, with the backing of Menelaus and the Jewish Hellenizers, issued decrees in Judaea obliging the population to abandon Jewish religious laws and practices. The Jewish Sanctuary was converted into a temple to Zeus and its inhabitants made to sacrifice to Greek deities [1 Macc 1.41-64].

The persecution led to a revolt that broke out in the Jewish village of Modi'in (Modein). A local Jewish priest, Mattathiah (Mattathias) the Hasmonaean, emphatically refused to sacrifice to Zeus. He slayed a Jew, who was about to offer a sacrifice, and also the administrative official charged with enforcing the decrees. To emphasise his zeal for the Torah, he instantly demolished the offending altar. Thereupon, Mattathiah and his five sons fled to the hills from where they carried out an insurgency, in which they were joined by a group of Asidaeans (*Hasidim* = "the righteous ones"). Accounts of their exploits are recorded in 1 Macc. 2.1-16.22; 2 Macc. 5.27-15.37; Josephus, *BJ* 1.36-54; *AJ* 12.265-13.229.

After Mattathiah's death about a year later, his third son, Judah (Judas) the Maccabee, led an army of Jewish insurgents to victory over the Seleucid armies. 1 Maccabees praises Judah's valour and military talent, suggesting that those qualities made Judah a natural choice for the new commander. Several explanations have been put forward for the epithet *Maccabaeus* which he acquired in the early days of the rebellion. Possibly this the name derives from the Aramaic *maqqaba* (*maqebet* in Modern Hebrew), "hammer" or "sledgehammer", in acknowledgement of his military prowess. Judah's strategy was to avoid any open engagement with the much larger and better equipped Seleucid army, and to resort to guerrilla warfare. The strategy proved highly effective, enabling Judah to win crucial early victories and build up a stock of weapons, captured from the enemy. The first of these victories was against a force led by Apollonius, the governor of Samaria. Apollonius was killed in this encounter and Judah took possession of his sword, using it thereafter [1 Macc. 3.10-13].

Judah's next major encounter was with Seron, the Seleucid commander in Syria, at the head of a much larger Seleucid army, not far from the pass of Beth-horon on the main road from the coast to Jerusalem. This attack was successfully repulsed by Judah. Lysias, whom Antiochus left as viceroy while he departed on his campaign against the Parthians, then dispatched a substantial force under the command of three generals, Ptolemy son of Dorymenes, Nicanor and Gorgias. The Seleucid army marched on Judaea and established their camp at Ammaus (Emmaus), at the foot of the Judaean hills. The Maccabaean fighters assembled at Mizpah, where they held a service of solemn worship and were then organised into a disciplined army. Forewarned that Gorgias was about to stage a surprise attack on the camp of the Jewish army during the hours of darkness, Judah led his men on a night march and succeeded in eluding Gorgias, While Gorgias was out searching for the Maccabees in the hills with part of his army, Judah launched a bold attack on the fortified Seleucid camp and scattered the enemy army. Having sustained a great loss of his fighting force, Georgias was obliged to withdraw [1 Macc. 3.13-4.25; cf. 2 Macc. 10.14-38].

In response to the defeat at Emmaus, Lysias returned with an even larger army to stamp out the Maccabaean insurgency. He marched it around the Judaean heartland, and then entered it from the direction of Idumaea, to the south, setting up camp at Beth-zur, between Hebron and Bethlehem. Judah launched a direct attack on Lysias' army, and his highly motivated troops succeeded in overwhelming the numerically superior enemy in the ensuing

Ill. 4.3 Map of the Seleucid Empire at the accession of Antiochus IV Epiphanes in 175 BCE.

battle close to Beth-zur. The tide in the struggle seemed to be turning in favour of the Maccabees, who were now poised to liberate Jerusalem [1 Macc. 4.28-36; 2 Macc. 11.1-15 (where the Maccabaean victory at Beth-zur is placed chronologically after the death of Antiochus IV and the recovery of Jerusalem and its Temple)].

Principal Ancient Sources:
1 Maccabees 1.10-6.16.
2 Maccabees 4.7-10.8 ; 11.1-15.
Daniel 7.8-25; 8.9-25; 11.30-39; 12.11.
Appian, *Syriaca* 39; 45; 66.
Cassius Dio, 20.
Diodorus Siculus, 29.32; 30.2, 7, 14-18; 31.1-2, 16-17; 34/35.1.
Eusebius, *Chronicon* p. 253.
Josephus, *Bellum Judaicum* (*BJ*) 1.31-54.
Josephus, *Antiquitates Judaicae* (*AJ*) 12.234-13.229; 15.41.
Josephus, *Contra Apionem* 2.80-84.
Livy, *Ab urbe condita* 40.8; 41.20, 24-25; 42.6, 14, 29, 34, 37-38; 44.14, 19, 24; 45.10-13, 44.
Livy, *Periochae* 41.5-6; 44.7; 45.2-3; 46.11.
Malalas 89.205.
Pliny, *Naturalis historia* 5.86, 93; 6.138-139, 147, 152.
Pausanias, 1.21; 5.12.
Polybius, 3.3, 26.1a-1; 28.1, 17-23; 29.2, 23-27; 30.25-27; 31.9, 11, 16-17.
Strabo, *Geographia* 9.1.
Tacitus, *Historiae* 5.8.

Il. 4.4. Antiochus IV Theos Epiphanes. AR tetradrachm (31 mm, 16.96 gm), struck c. 167-164 BCE. Ake-Ptolemais (Acre) mint. Diademed head of Antiochus IV, AB monogram behind / Zeus seated, holding a Nike with a wreath in his right hand and a sceptre in left; palm branch in outer left field. Two monograms in exergue. The Greek inscription reads ΒΑΣΙΛΕΩΣ ΑΝΤΙΟΧΟΥ ΘΕΟΥ ΕΠΙΦΑΝΟΥΣ ΝΙΚΗΦΟΡΟΥ, "of King Antiochos, god made manifest, the victorious". *SC* no.1476.2b.

This relatively late portrait depicts Antiochus as care-worn, perhaps reflecting his frustrated ambitions in Egypt, the rebellion against his rule in Judaea and the defection of Armenia and adjacent Media Atropatene from the Seleucid kingdom.

Ill. 4.5. View towards Beit Ur al-Fuqa (Upper Beth-horon) in an early 20th century photograph [PEF Photographic Archives, G483 (John Garstang, 1928); courtesy of the Palestine Exploration Fund, London]. Beth-horon comprised twin settlements, differentiated by the prefixes 'Lower' and 'Upper' [e.g. in Josh. 10.10], which guarded the two ends of a strategic defile followed by the ancient road to the Judean hill country and Jerusalem from the coastal plain, which can be seen in the background to the left. This pair of settlements was reputed to have been established by King Solomon [1 Kgs. 9.17; 2 Chron. 8.5]. The defile of Beth-horon was the scene of an epic battle fought by Judah the Maccabee in which his Jewish irregulars repulsed a Seleucid force under Seron [1 Macc. 3.16]. In those days the landscape was more verdant, with the hills and valleys cloaked in woodland.

THE TOBIAD MANSION AT TYROS, ACROSS THE JORDAN

During the Persian and Hellenistic periods, the region on the east bank of the Jordan, opposite Judaea was occupied by an Ammonite clan, headed by the house of Tobiah. Thus in the 5th century BCE, there is a Tobiah the Ammonite mentioned in the Book of Nehemiah (2.10, etc.) and a clan chieftain known as Toubias, an animal breeder for Ptolemy II, mentioned in several of the Greek Zenon Papyri in the mid-3rd century BCE.

Sometime during the reign of Seleucus IV, Hyrcanus, the head of the Ammonite-Jewish Tobiad clan embarked on the construction of a *baris* (palatial mansion) at Tyros (present-day 'Iraq al-'Amir) near the east bank of the Jordan in c. 180 BCE. His forebears crop up in ancient sources. According to Josephus [*AJ*, 12.228-37], the Tobiad *baris* was constructed in white stone and adorned with giant figures of animals. It had chambers for banqueting and sleeping, and was supplied with running water. It was set in parkland, with a lake. This description in Josephus has been strikingly confirmed by archaeological investigations of the monumental ruins of the Qasr al-'Abd at 'Iraq al-'Amir and the nearby rock-cut tombs, two of which bear the name "Tobiah" carved in Aramaic letters next to their entrances. The building is unfinished, which indicates that Hyrcanus did not complete it before he died. We are told by Josephus that the pro-Ptolemaic Hyrcanus fell out of favour with the Seleucid regime and he committed suicide after the accession of Antiochus IV in about 175 BCE.

Ill. 4.6. View of the palatial *baris* (the Qasr al-'Abd) after partial reconstruction using original masonry that had fallen. Courtesy of Professor Shimon Gibson.

Ill. 4.7. The name טוביה ("Tuvyah") cut into the side of a cave entrance in the cliff-face overlooking 'Iraq al-'Amir, 3rd century BCE

Ill. 4.8. Reconstruction of the palatial *baris* of Hyrkanos the Tobiad at 'Iraq al-'Amir, between Jericho and Amman (© F. Larché).

Ill. 4.9. Detail of lion frieze (lioness and cub), part of the monumental frieze of the Tobiad *baris* (Qasr al-'Abd); © Professor Shimon Gibson

Antiochus IV as a Patron of Greek Religion and Culture

Antiochus IV acquired the reputation of a benefactor of Greek cities and patron of Hellenic culture. He is praised by the historian Polybius, otherwise rather critical of this despotic king, for having behaved in a regal manner in two important respects — his benefactions to the Greek cities and the honours paid to the gods [Polybius, 26.1, 10-11; cf. Livy, *Ab urbe condita* 41.20.5-10]. He defrayed the building expenses for the Olympieion at Athens, honouring Olympian Zeus and contributing altars and statues at Delos. Antiochus also initiated the building of a temple to Zeus at Antioch [Livy, *Ab urbe condita* 41.20.9]. Judging from the quality and style of the workmanship, he was also probably responsible for the temple of Zeus Olbius at Uzunçaburc (Olbia) in Cilicia.

The devotion of Antiochus IV to Olympian Zeus is particularly noticeable on his coinage, where an enthroned Zeus, holding a winged victory in his right hand, facing outwards, and a sceptre in the other, takes the place of Apollo on the silver issues. The Zeus type is either a rendering of the colossal Zeus Nicephorus at Olympia, sculpted by Pheidias in gold and ivory (c. 449-438 BCE), which was one of the seven wonders of the ancient world [Pausanias, 5.10, 2; 11, 1], or it represents a closely modelled copy which served as a cult statue in Antioch. Zeus Nicephorus had already featured on some tetradrachms of the founder of the Seleucid dynasty, Seleucus I Nicator (as illustrated near the beginning of the book), so this subject was not a novelty on Seleucid coins. However, the Nike on the tetradrachms of Seleucus I faces inwards towards the deity, as it probably did at Olympia, rather than outwards as on the coins of Antiochus IV and his Seleucid successors.

Antiochus resided for some time in Athens as early as 178 BCE, some three years before he seized the Seleucid throne. This can help to account for the existence of statues to him in Athens by the time of his accession [Habicht 2006, 167].

Pausanias [5.12, 4] mentions a woollen curtain hung in the sanctuary of the temple of Zeus at Olympia. He says that this curtain was decorated by Assyrian weavers and dyed with Phoenician purple. It was presented by one Antiochus, who is widely identified with Antiochus IV, an ardent devotee of Olympian Zeus. In that case, this fabric may be a curtain of "fine linen and scarlet" (i.e. the veil of the Temple, a work of "Babylonian tapestry") that Antiochus plundered when the Jewish Sanctuary in Jerusalem was defiled and turned over to pagan worship [1 Macc. 1.22; Josephus, *BJ* 5.212-14; *AJ* 12.250; 15.394].

Ill. 4.10. Temple of Olympian Zeus in Athens, constructed in c. 170 BCE at the behest of Antiochus IV, some 350 years after the sons of the tyrant Pisistratus had initiated this project, and which had then been left in abeyance [Polybius, 26.1, 11; Livy, *Ab urbe condita* 41.20. 8; Strabo, *Geographia* 9.306; *Anthologia Palatina* 9.701-702]. Its architect was Roman, one Decimus Cossutius [Abramson 1975]. An inscription found close to the temple is inscribed in Greek with the name *Dekmos Kossoutios Popliou Romaios* [*IG*² 4099]. A graffito found in the Seleucid capital, Antioch, mentioning a Cossutius [*IGLS* 3.1, 825] may refer to one of this architect's descendants. http://en.wikipedia.org/wiki/List_of_Ancient_Greek_temples#mediaviewer/File:Temple_Of_Olmpian_Zeus_retouched.jpg. Courtesy Wikipedia and Creative Commons Org.

Antiochus' used his promotion of the cult of Olympian Zeus to forge standard religious and cultural practices – the two being closely interlinked – among the diverse peoples within the Seleucid kingdom. He exploited this policy to enhance his stature as a ruler, by projecting himself as Zeus "made manifest" (i.e. as the embodiment of this deity). Antiochus' intemperate behaviour in the political and religious spheres earned him the nickname *Epimanes* ("The Mad One"), a play on his epithet, Epiphanes [Polybius, 26.1, 1].

Ill. 4.11. Temple of Zeus Olbius at Uzunçaburc (Olbia), Cilicia, attributed to Antiochus IV. From http://tahsinsahin33.tripod.com/tarihce.htm.

ANTIOCHUS IV'S EGYPTIAN CAMPAIGN COINS

Sometime between autumn 169 and the following summer/autumn 168 BCE, a series of 'Egyptianising' coins, i.e. imitating Ptolemaic bronze coins in terms of their design types and denominations, but bearing the name and epithets of Antiochus IV, was minted, most probably in Antioch – they are mostly found in Syria. This issue must have been intended for circulation in Egypt in the wake of an anticipated Seleucid conquest of the Ptolemaic kingdom. It suggests that the invasion was well planned, but in the event it did not succeed for several reasons, not least Roman intervention (see below). These coins bear witness to what might have been.

Ill. 4.12. Antiochos IV Theos Epiphanes (175-164 BCE). Æ tetra-obol (34 mm, 38.07 gm). Antioch mint. Struck 169-168 BCE. Laureate head of Zeus-Serapis right, wearing taenia with Osiris cap at tip / Eagle standing on thunderbolt. The Greek inscription reads ΒΑΣΙΛΕΩΣ ΑΝΤΙΟΧΟΥ ΘΕΟΥ ΕΠΙΦΑΝΟΥΣ, "of King Antiochus, *Theou Epiphanous* (god made manifest)". *SC* 1413.

Ill. 4.13. Antiochus IV Theos Epiphanes. Æ diobol (26 mm, 17.66 gm). Wreathed head of Isis / Eagle standing on thunderbolt. The Greek inscription again reads [Β]ΑΣΙΛΕΩΣ ΑΝΤΙΟΧΟΥ ΘΕΟΥ [Ε]ΠΙΦΑΝΟΥΣ. *SC* 1414.

ANTIOCHUS IV AND THE OUTBREAK OF THE REBELLION

Simmering Tensions between the Seleucids and Rome

Following the crushing defeats of the Seleucid armies led by Antiochus III, by the Romans at Thermopylae (191 BCE) and Magnesia (190 BCE), followed by the crippling war indemnity levied on the defeated monarchy by the victors, the Seleucids were wary of provoking their rapidly growing rival in the west. The humiliation suffered by Antiochus III was repeated in 168 BCE outside Alexandria when the Roman envoy Gaius Popillius Laenas, delivered Rome's ultimatum to Antiochus IV to withdraw from Egypt.

This historic standoff finds an echo in the contrast between near-contemporary coins issued by the Roman Republic and Antiochus IV. Both dating from the mid-2nd century BCE, they feature the same subject, a *biga* being spurred on by a winged victory. The respective treatments of the motif in the two cases are characteristic of Hellenistic and Roman approaches to art. The Seleucid chariot group is monumental, statuesque and idealised, whereas that on the Roman coin is more expressive, with the figures and their poses reflecting everyday reality.

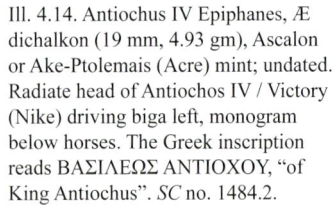

Ill. 4.14. Antiochus IV Epiphanes, Æ dichalkon (19 mm, 4.93 gm), Ascalon or Ake-Ptolemais (Acre) mint; undated. Radiate head of Antiochos IV / Victory (Nike) driving biga left, monogram below horses. The Greek inscription reads ΒΑΣΙΛΕΩΣ ΑΝΤΙΟΧΟΥ, "of King Antiochus". *SC* no. 1484.2.

The rays emanating from the head of Antiochus refer to the claim that he was a god.

Ill. 4.15. Roman Republic. AR denarius (20 mm, 3.76 gm). Rome mint: moneyer, L. Saufeius, 152 BCE. Helmeted head of Roma right, X behind / Victory driving biga to the right. The Latin inscription reads L.SAVF / ROMA. Crawford no. 204/1.

Victory driving a two-horse chariot, or biga, was a popular motif on Roman Republican coins issued in the 150s BCE. The "X" behind the head of Roma is a mark of value, ten asses for one denarius.

CHAPTER 5.

FROM ANTIOCHUS V TO TRYPHON – THE WARS OF THE MACCABEES

Antiochus V Eupator (164 - 162 BCE) [Grainger 1997, 27-28; *SC* 2.1, 127] was only nine when he succeeded to the Seleucid throne, according to Appian [*Syriaca* 46; 66]. Regent for the boy was the general Lysias, who had been left in charge of the western provinces by Antiochus IV. Antiochus V's reign was beset with difficulties. His guardian, Lysias, was seriously challenged by another member of Antiochus IV's entourage (or 'Friends'), Philip. By having to divert the Seleucid army to deal with Philip's insurrection, the attempt by Antiochus and Lysias to quash the Jewish rebellion ended in a weak compromise despite Seleucid success on the battlefield.

Next, there was interference by Rome. In 163 or 162, three Roman legates, led by Gnaeus Octavius (Consul in 165 BCE), were dispatched to Antioch with instructions to supervise Seleucid implementation of the Treaty of Apamea. Octavius ordered the Seleucid fleet to be burnt and the war elephants killed, but these actions caused outrage in the kingdom and Octavius was assassinated by some angry citizens of Laodicea. While all this was happening, Ptolemy, the Seleucid governor of Commagene, saw his opportunity to break free of control from Antioch and declared his independence.

Ill. 5.1. Antiochus V Eupator (164-162 BCE). AR tetradrachms (30 mm, 16.83 gm and 28 mm, 16.81 gm, respectively). Antioch mint. Diademed head of Antiochus V / Zeus seated, holding a Nike with a wreath in his right hand and a sceptre in his left; monogram in the outer left field. The Greek inscription reads ΒΑΣΙΛΕΩΣ ΑΝΤΙΟΧΟΥ ΕΥΠΑΤΟΡΟΣ, "of King Antiochus, *Eupatoros* (of a noble father)". (a) *Above*: *SC* no.1575.1; (b) *below*: *SC* no. 1575.2a.

The epithet "Eupator" is, of course, a reference to Antiochus IV. The promotion of the cult of Olympian Zeus was faithfully continued by Antiochus V.

FROM ANTIOCHUS V TO TRYPHON 51

Ill. 5.2. An oil lamp from the southern Levant, contemporary with the Maccabees, decorated with ovolo and chevron patterns, both popular dmotifs in architectural ornament of the period (mid-2nd century – early 1st century BCE)

To compound the misery of Antiochus V and his ruling circle, the king's uncle, Demetrius escaped forced exile in Rome and was acknowledged by the Seleucid army as its rightful monarch. The army handed over Antiochus and Lysias to Demetrius, who had them summarily executed. In time, Demetrius received recognition from the Roman Senate.

Judah entered the Holy City at the head of his army, without serious opposition. He and his followers immediately set about restoring and cleansing the derelict Temple, relighting the lamps on the lampstand (*menorah*) with ritually pure oil, and on the 25th of Kislev (14 December, 164 BCE) renewed the Temple services. "Then Judah, his brothers, and the whole congregation of Israel decreed that the rededication of the altar should be observed with joy and gladness at the same season each year, for eight days, beginning on the 25th of Kislev" [1 Macc. 4.26-59]. The date indicates that this event occurred after the accession of Antiochus V, as indicated by 2 Maccabees, although according to 1 Maccabees (and Josephus), it happened while his father was still alive.

Aware of the threat to Seleucid hold over Judaea posed by the unexpected Maccabaean victories, Lysias signalled that the Seleucid monarchy was willing to make an accommodation with the Maccabees. A letter from the Seleucid monarch to the Jewish people, reproduced in

Ill. 5.3. View of Hebron with the Tombs of the Patriarchs (Haram al-Khalil) visible in the middle distance, in a 19th century photograph [PEF Photographic Archives P2107 (Frank Mason Good, 1875); courtesy of the Palestine Exploration Fund, London]. Hebron, King David's first capital [1 Kgs. 2.11], located in the southern Judean hills, is the traditional burial place of Abraham, Isaac and Jacob, and their respective wives (apart from Rachel). It is notable for the splendid enclosure that Herod the Great constructed around the Cave of Machpelah (the Haram al-Khalil), which still dominates the town. Judah the Maccabee captured the town in his Idumaean campaign [1 Macc. 5.65].

2 Maccabees, declared an amnesty to the all the Judaeans who had been displaced by the fighting. This document seems have been drafted by Antiochus IV before his death, because it is dated to April 164 BCE.

With the liberation of Jerusalem (apart from the *Akra* fortress) and the rededication of the Temple temporarily achieved, Judah set out to consolidate his authority. Emboldened by their string of successes, the Maccabees sought more than toleration, raising their sights to full independence. Judah fortified the Temple Mount and the stronghold of Beth-zur. He launched attacks on neighbouring peoples, including the Idumaeans and Ammonites across the Jordan, "because they had hemmed Israel in". Judah also answered pleas from Jewish communities in Gilead and Galilee for help from provocations by their neighbours, with measures of practical help. He dispatched his younger brother, Simon *Thassi*, to

Galilee with 3,000 men where he carried out a successful series of military operations. Judah led the campaign in Transjordan himself, taking with him his brother Jonathan *Apphus*. In a series of battles, they defeated their foes and rescued their Jewish compatriots who had been incarcerated in fortified towns in Gilead. Many of these Jews and those of Galilee, evidently quite a small minority of the local population, were evacuated to Judaea (probably only temporarily). Following these campaigns, Judah made war on the Edomites in the south, capturing Hebron and razing its fortifications. He then marched his men through Marisa to the Mediterranean coast, pulling down altars and statues of the local gods in Azotus (Ashdod), and returned to Judaea laden with spoil. While the Maccabees were clocking up victories, two Jewish commanders, Joseph son of Zachariah and Azariah, decided to take an initiative on their own and launched an attack on the coastal town of Jamnia. There they were met in battle by Gorgias and were roundly defeated by his Seleucid troops [1 Macc. 4.60-5.68].

The Syrian garrison and other occupants of the *Akra* were harassing worshippers in the Temple, so Judah resolved to capture the fortress and laid siege to it. The besieged occupants appealed for help to Lysias, who was continuing to serve as the regent of the young king Antiochus V Eupator. Lysias and Antiochus Eupator embarked on a fresh offensive against the Maccabees. As in his first campaign, Lysias and his army wheeled around Judaea, entering it from the south, and laid siege to Beth-zur. Judah pulled his men from the encirclement of the *Akra* and went to meet Lysias. In the battle of Beth-zechariah, south of Bethlehem, Eleazar *Avaran*, one of the Maccabee brothers, identified a war elephant that carried, or so he mistakenly presumed, the Seleucid King Antiochus V, on account of the special armour the elephant wore. He decided to risk his life and attacked the elephant from below, thrusting a spear into its belly. The elephant collapsed on him, dead, killing him too. Despite its heroic effort, the smaller Jewish army was defeated in the battle, giving the Seleucids their first major victory over the Maccabees. Judah and his men were forced to withdraw to Jerusalem [1 Macc. 6.18-48].

The inhabitants of Beth-zur had no food to enable them to resist Lysias and decided to surrender. The latter reached Jerusalem, laying siege to the city. The defenders were in the grip of a famine because it was a sabbatical year, when the fields had been left uncultivated so that the food stores were empty. Jerusalem was saved from being recaptured by the Seleucids by the sudden withdrawal of Lysias and Antiochus Eupator forced by the return of Philip with the late king Antiochus IV's expeditionary force from Persia and Media. Shortly before he died, Antiochus IV had appointed Philip as regent for his young son. Philip was now attempting to take possession of

Antioch. In disengaging from his campaign against the Maccabees, Lysias proposed a peace settlement, which was concluded at the end of 163 BCE. The terms of the peace agreement included the restoration of religious freedom, permitting the Jews to live in accordance with their own laws and giving official recognition of their repossession of the Temple. A letter from Antiochus V setting out these terms is contained in 2 Macc. 11.22-26. Judah accepted this offer and Lysias headed back to Antioch after giving orders to demolish Jerusalem's fortifications. On arrival at Antioch, Lysias confronted Philip and took the Seleucid capital by storm. Menelaus had lent his support to the offensive waged by Lysias and Antiochus V against the Maccabees, believing that this course would help maintain him in his high priestly office. Lysias saw through Menelaus' stratagems and charged him with responsibility for the conflict in Judaea. Antiochus V ordered his arrest. He was taken under guard to Beroea (modern Aleppo) in Syria and made to suffer an agonising death there [1 Macc. 6.48-63; 2 Macc. 13].

Principal Ancient Sources:
1 Maccabees 4.26-5.68, 6.17-7.4.
2 Maccabees 9.29; 10.10-14.1.
Appian, *Syriaca* 45-47.
Cassius Dio, 20.25.
Eusebius, *Chronicon* p.253.
Josephus, *Bellum Judaicum* (*BJ*) 1.40-47
Josephus, *Antiquitates Judaicae* (*AJ*) 12.295-296, 360-390; 20.234-235.
Livy, *Periochae* 46.11-12.
Pliny, *Naturalis historia* 34.24.
Polybius, 31.2, 11-13.

Greek-speaking Sidonian communities bordering Judaea in the second century BCE

An inscription found in December 1986 at the site of the ancient port of Jamnia (present-day Yavneh Yam), south of Jaffa, contains two letters, written in Greek, between the citizens of Yavneh Yam with the Greek King Antiochus V Eupator. This correspondence indicates that these citizens tried, by way of rendering services (or by merely paying lip service), to extract special favours from the young monarch.

The first letter is a petition to King Antiochus from the Sidonians in the port of Jamnia: "Since [their ancestors] rendered many services to his grandfather, promptly obeying [all] instructions regarding the naval service..." The "grandfather" is presumably Antiochus III, whom the city would have helped during his war against the Ptolemies in Egypt.

The second letter is by the King who writes to a particular citizen of Jamnia-on-the-Sea, called Nessos; perhaps he was the writer of the petition, or he was the representative of the city. It states: "[King An]tiochus to Nessos, greetings. The recorded petition was submitted by [the Sid]onians [in Jamnia]. Since ... the ... referred to are [also] immune ... so that they will also enjoy the same privileges. Farewell. Loos 149". Loos is the name of the 10th month and 149th

Ill. 5.4. Inscription recording correspondence between the Sidonians at Jamnia-on-the-Sea and Antiochus V Eupator. Courtesy of the Israel Antiquities Authority.

year according to the Seleucid era, so the date given is early Spring of 163 BCE. The Sidonians of Jamnia were evidently of Phoenician stock, like the Sidonians of nearby Marisa (see below). In both cases, these Sidonian communities were purveyors of Hellenic culture throughout the southern Levant; see Isaac1991, 132-44.

The Hellenistic town of Marisa occupied the two uppermost strata of Tell Sandahannah, situated 62 km south-west from Jerusalem by road. The tell was the site of Biblical Mareshah, and there are extensive remains of the Iron Age town on lower strata. Excavations over the last century have brought to light two phases of construction in the Hellenistic period, the earlier dated to c. 300 BCE and the later, more extensive walled town has been dated to the early 2nd century BCE. A large quantity of pottery, including numerous Rhodian amphora handles, sculptural fragments and an inscribed statue base, with a dedication to Arsinoe III, sister and consort of Ptolemy IV Philopator (221/0-204 BCE) have been found there.

The tell is surrounded by a large number of subterranean burial chambers, cisterns olive presses, *columbaria*, storerooms from the Hellenistic period, including a few remarkable painted catacombs. One of these, Tomb 1, was the burial place of prominent members of a Sidonian community settled at Marisa.

Ill. 5.5. Photograph and transcription of the graffito epitaph to "Apollophanes, son of Sesmaios, 33 years head of the Sidonians at Marisa, reputed the best and most kin-loving of all those of his time; he died, having lived 74 years". This inscription was to be seen on a lintel above a burial chamber in Tomb 1 at Marisa, as shown here, until the period between the two World Wars, when it was cut out and has disappeared.

Tomb I was decorated in Graeco-Egyptian style typical of the Ptolemaic period, and painted with a frieze of a leopard hunt (shown below) and a sequence of different wild animals.

Ill. 5.6. Painted scene of a leopard hunt in Tomb I at Marisa, showing a mounted huntsman, accompanied by trumpeter and dogs, attacking a female leopard.

The numerous tomb inscriptions have furnished sufficient information regarding the interrelationship between many of those interred in this tomb cave to enable to enable a family tree to be reconstructed. In general, the names of the first generation are Semitic, including Sesmaios which is Phoenician, while those of their offspring are mostly Greek. In the third and fourth generation, we find Idumaean names including Babas, Babatas, Sabo, Qosbanos and Qosnatanos (incorporating the theophorous prefix "Qos", the Idumaean chief deity), attesting to the assimilation of the Sidonian family into the population among which they settled. The dates given in several of the inscriptions are according to the Seleucid era and span the years 196 to 119 BCE.

The paintings and inscriptions found in this tomb at Marisa bear witness to the ubiquitous Sidonian / Phoenician trading communities acting as disseminators of Hellenic culture in the Levant during the period of Ptolemaic and Seleucid dominance of the area.

Demetrius I Soter (162 - 150 BCE) [Grainger 1997, 39-42; *SC* 2.1, 261-63] arrived in Tripolis (present-day Tripoli in the Lebanon) with a company of mercenaries in the autumn of 162 BCE to claim the Seleucid throne, after escaping from Roman detention with the help of friends, including the historian Polybius. He received a hospitable welcome from the Syrian population and set about stamping his authority on the Seleucid kingdom.

Within a few months he was obliged to deal with a revolt in the east by the governor or satrap of Media, Timarchus. This satrap, who had distinguished himself by defending Media against the emergent Parthians, used Demetrius' accession as an excuse to declare his own sovereignty and extend his realm into Babylonia. His forces were however insufficient to succeed against Demetrius, who defeated and killed Timarchus in 161 BCE. Demetrius acquired the epithet of *Soter*, or "Saviour", from the Babylonians, who he delivered from subjugation by Timarchus. At about this time, Demetrius wedded his own sister, Laodice, who had returned to Syria after the demise of her previous husband, Perseus of Macedon, in 167 BCE.

He was sucked into a fruitless dynastic conflict in Cappadocia, between two warring brothers and made an abortive attempt to bribe the Ptolemaic governor of Cyprus to switch his allegiance from Alexandria to Antioch. Demetrius was also drawn into a new phase of warfare in Judaea by responding to the intrigues of the High Priest in Jerusalem, Alcimus. His incompetent handling of political affairs, both external and internal, opened a rift between Demetrius and many of his subjects. Demetrius' downfall is attributed to Heracleides, a surviving brother of the defeated rebel Timarchus, who championed the cause of Alexander *Balas*, a boy he claimed was a natural son of Antiochus IV Epiphanes. Gaining the support of Ptolemy VI Philometor of Egypt (c. 180-145 BCE) and his army, Alexander was landed Ake-Ptolemais (present-day Acre), which readily surrendered to him. Realising that a showdown with *Balas* and his formidable forces was imminent, Demetrius spirited his two infant sons to Cnidus and prepared to face his adversary, whose power rapidly increased through the defection of many soldiers of the Seleucid army. When the two parties joined in battle, in 150 BCE, Demetrius was defeated and killed.

ll. 5.7. Demetrius I Soter (162-150 BCE). AR tetradrachm (29 mm,16.73 gm). Struck in year SE 160 (ΞP) = 153/152 BCE. Antioch mint. Diademed head of Demetrius I, within a wreath of laurel / Tyche sitting on a throne borne by a winged female creature with a serpentine tail. The deity holds a cornucopia in her left hand and a short sceptre in her right; two monograms in the outer left field, and date in exergue. The Greek inscription reads ΒΑΣΙΛΕΩΣ ΔΗΜΗΤΡΙΟΥ ΣΩΤΗΡΟΣ, "of King Demetrius *Soter* (the saviour)". *SC* no. 1641.5a.

Demetrius' favouring of Tyche on his coinage was in appreciation of his good fortune in his meteoric rise from a hostage in Rome to sovereign of the Seleucid kingdom. On this and on many other tetradrachms of Demetrius, the usual bead-and-reel border, customary on Antiochene tetradrachms from the reign of Antiochus III, is replaced by a laurel wreath for reasons that are not entirely clear. The laurel was sacred to Apollo, the patron deity of the Seleucid dynasty from its foundation, but a wreath of this plant was customarily held to be an expression of victory in the Hellenic world.

Alcimus (Yakim), the erstwhile leader of the Hellenizing party in Jerusalem paid court to the new king, Demetrius Soter, at the head of a delegation of his supporters, complaining about the Maccabees, accusing them of persecuting loyal followers of the Seleucid monarchy among the Jews. He urged the king to send a trusted officer to punish the Maccabees and their supporters. Demetrius acceded to this request, assigning the task to Bacchides, a member of the royal circle and hitherto Seleucid governor of the territory beyond the Euphrates. Alcimus was appointed High Priest by the king, in preferment to Onias, the son or nephew of the murdered High Priest of the same name. Sensing that he was in mortal danger, this Onias (referred to in the literature as Onias IV), fled with his followers to Egypt, where he was hospitably received by Ptolemy VI Philometor. Ptolemy invited Onias to settle at Leontopolis in the Nile delta (present-day Tell al-Yehudieh), where he established a Jewish temple, where sacrifices were conducted until it was ordered to be closed down by Vespasian in 73 CE, three years after the destruction of the Jerusalem Temple by his son Titus [Josephus, *BJ* 1.190; 7.421-36; *AJ* 12.387-388; 13.62-73; 20.236]

Meanwhile, Alcimus was instructed to accompany Bacchides and a large military detachment to Judaea. Alcimus feigned conciliation with the Hassidim (Asidaeans), or Jewish pietists who had been supporting the Maccabees, but when their guard was down, he treacherously put 60 of their number to death. Despite the military backing he received from Bacchides, Alcimus encountered stiff resistance, although the Maccabees were forced out of Jerusalem [1 Macc. 7.1-24; 2 Macc. 14.3-4].

Finding that he was scarcely making any headway, Alcimus asked the king for more robust support. In response, Demetrius sent one of his most distinguished commanders, Nicanor, with the order to eliminate the Maccabees. The latter got the better of Nicanor's troops in their first encounter near Capharsalama. Returning to Jerusalem in a rage, Nicanor vowed to destroy the Temple unless Judah and his army surrendered to him. The rival armies clashed in battle at Adasa in northern Judaea in Adar (February) 161 BCE. Despite being vastly outnumbered by their foe, the Maccabees delivered Nicanor's army a crushing defeat and then pursued and cut down the fugitives. The head and arm were cut off Nicanor's corpse and displayed at Jerusalem, which was reoccupied by the Maccabees, and an annual festival, Nicanor Day, was instituted to celebrate this truly miraculous victory [1 Macc. 7.25-50; 2 Macc. 14.4-15.37; Scroll of Ta'anit 30].

In the wake of this success, Judah sent a delegation to Rome led by Eupolemus son of Yohanan (John) and Jason son of Eleazar, with the request for an alliance. The outcome of the mission was less than Judah had hoped for, the Romans committing themselves only to such obligations as were in their own interests, while demanding allegiance from the Jews. A letter dispatched by the Senate to Demetrius, forbidding him to act in a hostile manner against the Jews, failed to sway him [1 Macc. 8.1-32].

On receiving the news of Nicanor's defeat, Demetrius dispatched another armed expedition, once again commanded by Bacchides with an army said to number 20,000 men. Intimidated by such a large force, most of Judah's men quit the field of battle and urged their leader to do likewise for the good of their common cause. However, Judah stood firm and faced the enemy. In the Battle of Elasa (161/0 BCE), Judah and those who remained with him were killed. His body was collected from the battlefield by his brothers and later buried in the family sepulchre at Modi'in. Bacchides and his Seleucid army reoccupied Jerusalem: it would be almost a decade before the Maccabaean party would regain the Holy City [1 Macc. 9.1-22].

Jonathan succeeded as leader of the Maccabaean party from c. 160 to 143/2 BCE [1 Macc. 9.1-31]. He was given the surname *Apphus* (in Syriac, "the dissembler" or "the diplomat"), referring to one of his conspicuous talents [1 Macc. 2.5].

Encouraged by his victory, Bacchides handed control of Judaea to the Hellenizers and he made plans to eliminate the Maccabaean leadership, beginning with Jonathan, Judah's successor. To make matters worse for the Maccabees, a severe famine broke out in the land of Israel. News of Bacchides intentions reached Jonathan and his supporters. As a precaution he and his brother Simon *Thassi*, together with some of their comrades in arms, took refuge in the Wilderness of Thekoe (Tekoa), setting up camp near the 'pool of Asphar'. Jonathan gave the baggage of his party to his brother John, who took a small force and headed towards friendly Nabataeans. The plan was to hand over their baggage to the Nabataeans so as to give the Maccabees greater mobility but the "sons of Jambri of Medeba", evidenty a hostile clan, ambushed John and his team during their journey. John and his companions were killed and their cargo was looted. Soon after this incident, the Maccabaean brothers received information that one of the sons of Jambri was leading home a noble bride in great pomp, and saw their opportunity for taking revenge. They proceeded to Medeba, ambushed the bridal procession, killed the entire party, numbering about 300, and seized all their valuables [1 Macc. 9.32-42]. When news of this episode reached Bacchides, he led a large force down to the banks of the Jordan in pursuit of the Maccabees.

Most of Jonathan's men managed to disengage from combat with Bacchides' army, escaping by swimming across the Jordan to the eastern bank. Although this engagement resulted in a Maccabaean retreat, Bacchides lost about 1,000 men that day. On his return to Jerusalem, Bacchides fortified and garrisoned the several of the principal bastions in northern Judaea and southern Samaria, where the Hasmonaeans had been particularly active, as well as the towns of Beth-zur and Gazara (Gezer). He also interned the sons of leading Judaean families as hostages in the *Akra*, which was strongly reinforced at that time [1 Macc. 9.43-53].

After giving orders for the ancient wall of the inner court of the Temple to be demolished, Alcimus suffered a stroke and died in 159 BCE. Bacchides returned to the Seleucid capital, probably convinced that the opponents of the Maccabees were securely in control of Judaea. To be sure, the leaders of the Hellenizing party hatched a plan to capture Jonathan and his men in a night operation, but news of it leaked out and Maccabees managed to remain at large. Jonathan and his supporters made their way to a ruined fortress in the Judaean Desert, at a site called Beth-basi, generally identified with Khirbet Beit-bassa, 5 km north-east of Tekoah, which they refortified. After about two years, Bacchides arrived with siege engines and tried to capture the Maccabaean redoubt. The defenders fought back so fiercely that Bacchides had to abandon the siege. Then he returned to Syria, probably to deal with other emergencies that were engulfing the Seleucid kingdom. Jonathan saw an opportunity to strike a peace deal and sent envoys to Bacchides proposing a cessation of hostilities and an exchange of prisoners, which was accepted. Jonathan was able to set up a Maccabaean administration in Machmas (Michmash). There he "began to govern the people, rooting the godless out of Israel" [1 Macc. 9.54-73].

Jonathan evidently used this truce to good advantage, because his party grew in strength. An important external event advanced the Maccabaean cause still further, namely the bid of Alexander *Balas* for the Seleucid throne. Demetrius eagerly sought the support of Jonathan, permitting him to recruit an army and the garrison of the *Akra* in Jerusalem yielded up the Jewish prisoners that had been held there. Jonathan proceeded to take up residence at Jerusalem and also took steps to fortify the city. Demetrius' rival, Alexander *Balas* offered Jonathan more advantageous terms, including the appointment as High Priest of the Jews. The combination of office of ruler and high priest was not exceptional to Judaea, but conformed to a pattern encountered elsewhere in the Hellenistic world, including Ituraea (or Chalcis ad Libanum), to the north of Galilee.

Withdrawing his support from Demetrius, who could not be trusted, and declaring his allegiance to Alexander, Jonathan was the first member of his family to gain the high priesthood. Thereby, Jonathan became the official leader of his people and the Hellenizing party could no longer attack him without heavy consequences. On the Feast of Tabernacles of 153 or 152 BCE, Jonathan donned the High Priest's vestments and officiated in the Temple for the first time. It is unknown whom Jonathan replaced as High Priest, although it is possible that the post had remained vacant after the demise of Alcimus. In an attempt to win back Jonathan's loyalty, Demetrius undertook to lift tribute and taxes on Judaea, and to hand over the *Akra* in Jerusalem. Events justified Jonathan's decision to stand by Alexander *Balas*, for not long afterwards Demetrius lost his throne and life [1 Macc. 9.74-10.50].

Ill. 5.8. Wadi Suwenit (Michmash) [PEF Photographic Archives P3982 (H. H. Kitchener, 1874); courtesy of the Palestine Exploration Fund, London]. Wadi Suweinit is a deep gorge that descends from the Judaean hill country into the Jordan Valley near Jericho, passing immediately to the south of the biblical town of Michmash (identified with the present village of Mukhmas). According to the Bible, shortly after Saul had been anointed king, the Philistines struck deep into Israelite territory, reaching the pass of Mishmash, where they were surprised by the sudden appearance here of Saul's son, Jonathan [1 Sam. 13.5-14.31]. Michmash was resettled after the return from the Babylonian Exile [Ezra 2.27]. Jonathan the Hasmonaean chose this place for his residence after defeating a Seleucid army commanded by Bacchides [1 Macc. 9.73].

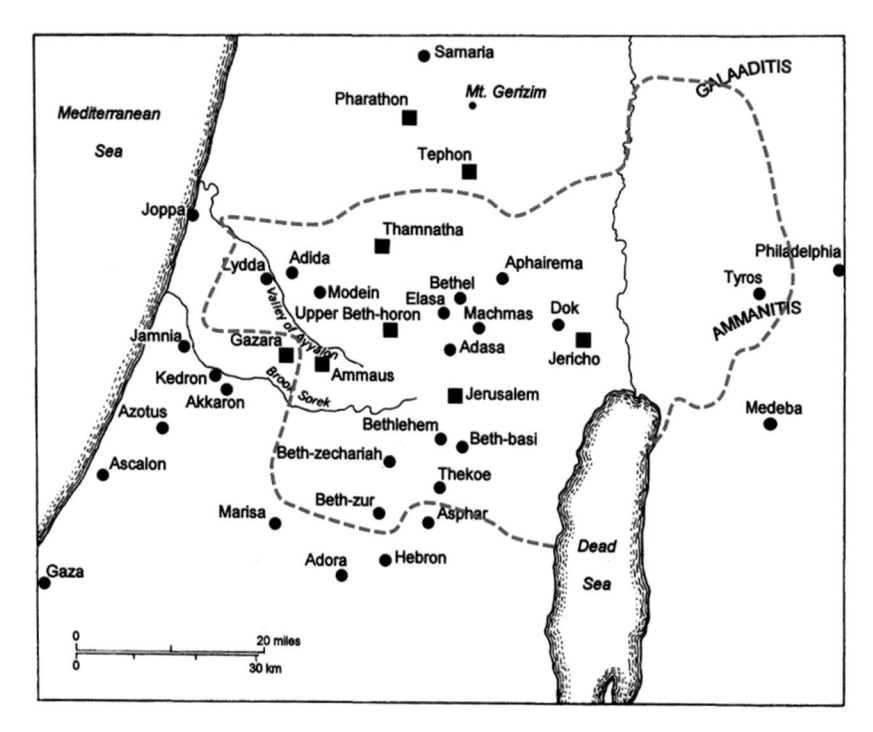

Ill. 5.9. Judaea during the wars of the Maccabees, showing its borders after the conquests of Jonathan *Apphus*, in 143/2 BCE. The squares represent the sites fortified by Bacchides in 160/59 BCE; after Goldstein 1990, fig. 1, p. 297.

Principal Ancient Sources:
1 Maccabees 2.5, 7-10.
2 Maccabees 14.-15.
Appian, *Syriaca* 45, 47;
Diodorus Siculus 31.18, 27a-30, 32a.
Eusebius, *Chronicon* pp.253-255.
Josephus, *Bellum Judaicum* (*BJ*) 1.190; 7.421-36
Josephus, *Antiquitates Judaicae* (*AJ*) 12.387-13.73; 20.236.
Justin, *Epitome* 34.3; 35.1-2
Livy, *Periochae* 46.11-12; 47.7; 48.27; 49.21, 27; 50.4; 52.10.
Polybius, 31.2, 11-15; 32.2-3, 10; 33.5, 15, 18-19.

Ill. 5.10. Demetrius I Soter. Æ trichalkon (19 mm, 6.86 gm). Tyre mint. Dated 159/8 BCE. Diademed head of Demetrios I / Stern of a Phoenician galley with a rudder; The Greek inscription reads ΒΑΣΙΛΕΩΣ ΔΗΜΗΤΡΙΟΥ LΔNP, ΤΥΡΙΩΝ, "of King Demetrius, SE 154 (159/8 BCE), of Tyre" and לצר ("of Tyre", in Phoenician script) in exergue. *SC* no. 1671.

This coin highlights the importance of the Phoenician coastal cities and their maritime trade to the economic life of the Seleucid Empire. These cities, in particular Sidon, Tyre and Ake-Ptolemais (Acre), figured prominently in the affairs of the Seleucid court after the reign of Antiochus III. They were allowed a semi-autonomous existence and flourished, minting their own silver and bronze coins. Many of the coin types carry maritime themes, including a galley, aphlaston or aplustre (its upward curving stern), prow, rudder, etc. The Phoenicians were renowned for their maritime feats and sea trading. Their warships were long and had a fairly shallow-draft, having prows tipped with a sturdy bronze ram. Phoenician vessels and their crews constituted an important element in the armed forces of the Persians and their successors in the Levant.

Ill. 5.11. A bronze ram weighing nearly half a tonne from a Phoenician warship, found at Athlit, is exhibited in the maritime museum in Haifa. There are four Greek symbols depicted in relief on this splendid bronze casting, Poseidon's trident, a Dioscuri cap surmounted with a star, an eagle's head (referring to Zeus), and Hermes' caduceus (*kerykeion*). They are the familiar attributes of the deities who safeguard ships and protect seamen. It is believed that this ram dates from between about 204 and 164 BCE. Courtesy of the Israel Antiquities Authority.

Alexander I Theopator Euergetes *Balas*
(152-145 BCE) [Grainger 1997, 6-7; *SC* 2.1, 209-10] was said to be a native of Smyrna, but groomed as a claimant to the Seleucid throne by Attalus II of Pergamon out of hostility to Demetrius Soter, which was reciprocated. He, Heracleides (brother of Timarchus) and others promoted his claim to be a son of Antiochus IV Epiphanes and rightful heir to the Seleucid throne. His popular epithet, *Balas*, from the Semitic title, *Ba'al*, meaning 'lord,' was not employed officially.

With Rome behind him and gaining the active support of Ptolemy VI of Egypt,

Ill. 5.12. Alexander I *Balas* (152-145 BCE). AR tetradrachms (26 mm, 14.17 and 30 mm, 16.52 gm, respectively). Diademed head of Alexander I. (a) *Above*: Sidon mint. Reverse: Eagle standing with a palm branch behind; FΞP (date) – SE 165 (148/7 BC) to the left, ΣΙΔΩ (Sido[n]) to the right. *SC* no. 1830.4.

Henceforth, the Phoenician coastal cities, including Tyre and Sidon regularly struck tetradrachms of this type, namely, to the lighter Egyptian weight standard (~ 14 gm) and to a Ptolemaic design (i.e. portraying an eagle on the reverse), probably to promote their strong and longstanding trade links with Egypt.

(b) *Below*: Antioch mint. Reverse: Zeus seated, holding a Nike offering a wreath in his right hand and a sceptre in his left; monograms in exergue. The Greek inscription reads ΒΑΣΙΛΕΩΣ ΑΛΕΞΑΝΔΡΟΥ (right) ΘΕΟΠΑΤΟΡΟΣ ΕΥΕΡΓΕΤΟΥ (left), "of King Alexander, *Theopatoros Euergetou* (the divinely fathered benefactor)". *SC* no. 1781.1h.

Alexander's epithet "Theopator Euergetes" is a reference to Alexander's claim to be a son of the deified Antiochus IV. The expressive and highly idealised portrait of Alexander *Balas*, with deep set eyes, upward gaze and free-flowing locks of hair, on this second piece bears a close stylistic affinity to some of the heads of sculpted figures, especially Athena's opponent, on the Great Altar of Pergamon (in the east section of the Gigantomachy frieze; see central inset), dedicated sometime between 188 and 139 BCE and considered to be one of the great masterpieces of 'proto-baroque' Hellenistic art.

Alexander landed at Ake-Ptolemais and won over the local Seleucid garrison. For two years, he and Demetrius I jockeyed for supremacy. Alexander spent the time establishing his power base, negotiating an alliance with the Maccabees, recruiting mercenaries and winning over deserters from Demetrius' army. The two rivals met on the battlefield in the summer of 150 BCE where Demetrius met his death. Having attained mastery of the Seleucid kingdom, Alexander requested a marriage alliance with Ptolemy VI Philometor of Egypt, which was granted. In 150 BCE, the royal wedding was held amid considerable pomp at Ake-Ptolemais with both kings in attendance, in which Alexander received the hand of Ptolemy's eldest daughter, Cleopatra Thea (born c.164 BCE). This Cleopatra was destined to be wedded to two other Seleucid kings, Demetrius II and Antiochus VII, and to be mother to no less than four future Seleucid monarchs, Antiochus VI (by Alexander *Balas*), Seleucus V and Antiochus VIII (by Demetrius II), and Antiochus IX (by Antiochus VII). This royal wedding was commemorated on a very rare issue of Seleucid tetradrachms struck at Ake-Ptolemais.

Alexander is reputed to have been a somewhat indolent and pleasure-seeking ruler who delegated the task of governing to members of his entourage. During his reign, the Seleucid kingdom sustained major losses of territory, with the Parthians conquering Media and Elymaïs encroaching on Seleucid territory under its able king, Kamnaskires I. In 147 BCE, a more serious threat to Alexander's rule materialised in the form of the future Demetrius II, son of Demetrius I, who landed in Cilicia with a contingent of mercenaries from Crete. Taking encouragement from this development, the population of Antioch rose up against Alexander, who withdrew his forces to Cilicia. Meanwhile, Ptolemy VI had arrived in Antioch with an army. As the Seleucids rallied to Demetrius, Ptolemy recognised Alexander's growing weakness and switched his support to the new king. Alexander was defeated in the battle of Antioch (145 BCE), also referred to as the battle of the Oenoparus. Alexander *Balas* fled for refuge to a Nabataean clan chief, who murdered him and sent his head to Ptolemy VI Philometor. The latter had himself been mortally wounded in the battle of Antioch and died shortly thereafter. The Egyptian garrisons that Ptolemy had left behind in Syria were liquidated or expelled by the local inhabitants, leaving the young Demetrius II take full control of the Seleucid kingdom.

> Jonathan was invited to the wedding of Alexander *Balas* and Cleopatra Thea in Ake-Ptolemais, but he arrived in time to participate in the post-nuptual feasting. He appeared with presents for both kings and was asked to sit between them as their equal; *Balas* even clothed him with his own royal robe and otherwise accorded him high honour. He would not listen to the Hellenizing party that continued to blacken Jonathan, but appointed the Jewish leader *strategos* (general) and *meridarches* (tributary ruler) of the

Seleucid kingdom and sent him back with honours to Jerusalem [1 Macc. 10.60-66].

Jonathan remained beholden to Alexander *Balas*. In 147 BCE, Demetrius II Nicator, son of Demetrius I Soter, appeared as a rival to *Balas*. Apollonius Taos, governor of Coele-Syria was probably supporting Demetrius' claim to rule and challenged Jonathan to a military engagement. Jonathan and Simon led a force of 10,000 men against Joppa (Jaffa) where the forces of Apollonius were gathered. Not expecting an attack so soon, the residents of Joppa were not prepared for a siege. The gates of the town were opened to the Maccabaean forces out of fear. However, Apollonius received reinforcements from Azotus (Ashdod) and appeared in the plain in charge of 3,000 men. The Seleucid forces were clearly outnumbered but Apollonius was relying on his superior cavalry and forced Jonathan to join him in battle. Jonathan attacked, storming, capturing and burning Azotus along with its temple of Dagon and the surrounding villages [1 Macc. 10.67-87].

As a reward for Jonathan's victory over his rival's army, Alexander *Balas* granted him the city of Ekron along with its outlying territory. The people of Azotus complained to King Ptolemy VI, who had come to make war against his son-in-law Alexander *Balas*, that Jonathan had destroyed their city and temple. Jonathan received Ptolemy civilly at Joppa and accompanied him northwards as far as the River Eleutherus in Phoenicia. He then returned to Jerusalem, maintaining peaceful relations with the King of Egypt despite their support for rival contenders for the Seleucid throne [1 Macc. 10.88-11.8].

Ill. 5.13. View south towards the town and harbour of Jaffa, in the 19th century [PEF Photographic Archives, P617 (Henry Phillips, 1866)]. There was already a significant urban settlement at Jaffa by the 14th century BCE, when it was under Egyptian control. It prospered as a trading port and, according to the Bible, cedar wood imported from the Lebanon was brought ashore there for Solomon's Temple [2 Chron. 2.16] and again when the Temple was rebuilt after the end of the Babylonian captivity [Ezra 3.7]. In the Persian period, Jaffa was occupied by Sidonians and it was the first sea port to be captured by the Maccabees (in 144 BCE). Simon expelled its gentile inhabitants and settled it with his own veterans [1 Macc. 10.76, 12.33-34, 13.11, 14.5].

Ill. 5.14. Alexander I *Balas* and Cleopatra Thea. AR tetradrachm (32 mm, 16.85 gm), Seleucia Pieria mint, c. 150 BCE. Jugate diademed busts of Cleopatra, wearing a *kalathos* and veil, and Alexander; in field left, A above a cornucopia / Zeus seated, holding a Nike, facing frontally, in his right hand and a sceptre in his left. The Greek inscription reads ΒΑΣΙΛΕΩΣ ΑΛΕΞΑΝΔΡΟΥ (right) ΘΕΟΠΑΤΟΡΟΣ ΕΥΕΡΓΕΤΟΥ (left). *SC* no. 1841. Numismatica Ars Classica (NAC) Auction 29 (11 May 2005), lot 220; courtesy of Numismatica Ars Classica NAC AG.

The *kalathos* (*modius* in Latin) is a cylindrical vase for containing grain, normally worn as a headdress by Egyptian queens as a mark of fertility. The cornucopia is another symbol of fecundity favoured by Egyptian monarchs. This double portrait is akin to a modern wedding photograph.

SC term*	Size, weight	Likely denominational value
A	22-29 mm, 11.0-24.3 gm	*octochalkon* (= 1 *obol* = $1/6$ *drachm*)
B	17-26 mm, 5.5-9.3 gm	*tetrachalkon* (*hemiobol*)
C	15-21 mm, 3.0-3.5 gm	*dichalkon*
D	12-14 mm, 1.5-3.0 gm	*chalkon*
E	8-11 mm, 0.6-1.0 gm	*hemichalkon*

* *SC* 2.2, table on p. 52.

Table 5.1. Bronze fractional denominations in Phoenicia from 198 BCE, and elsewhere in the Seleucid kingdom from the reign of Alexander I *Balas*.

From the coin evidence it has been deduced that the Seleucid kingdoms adopted an Attic system of denominations, with eight *chalkoi* to the *obolos* (obol) and six *oboloi* to the *drachmé* (drachm); see *SC* 2.2, p. 49

Principal Ancient Sources:
1 Maccabees 10-11.19.
Athenaeus, 211A.
Diodorus Siculus, 31.32a; 32.9c-10.2; 33.3.
Eusebius, Chronicon p. 255.
Josephus, *Antiquitates Judaicae* (*AJ*) 13.35-61, 80-87, 103-119.
Justin, *Epitome* 35.2
Livy, *Periochae* 50.4; 52.10-11.
Polybius, 33.15, 18

Demetrius II (first reign, 146 – 138 BCE) [Grainger 1997, 42-44; *SC* 2.1, 261-63], with the epithets **Theos Philadelphus Nicator**, was the middle son of Demetrius I Soter. No sooner had Demetrius II reclaimed the Seleucid throne with the help of Ptolemy VI Philometor, the Egyptian king had his daughter divorce Alexander *Balas* and remarried her to Demetrius II. He was just fifteen years of age and about three years Cleopatra's junior. They had three children together, a Seleucus (who reigned very briefly as Seleucus V), a daughter Laodice and the future Antochus VIII.

The immature king was quick to make himself unpopular. He laid off a substantial number of regular soldiers and cut the pay of the rest, while bolstering his mercenary force. The people of Syria were alienated by the poor conduct of the youthful Demetrius, and his sustaining force of Cretan mercenaries under Lasthenes. An uprising by the inhabitants of Antioch, precipitated by the pillaging by these mercenaries was brutally crushed, with the aid of a detachment soldiers sent by Jonathan from Judaea, and this only intensified hatred for him among the population of Syria. The mood of growing disaffection was used by Diodotus, an officer who had served under Alexander *Balas*, to instigate a rebellion in the name of the latter's infant son, Antiochus. The rebel army triumphed over Demetrius, obliging him to flee to Cilicia. Diodotus, now calling himself Tryphon, and his young charge, Antiochus VI, took control of Antioch and Ake-Ptolemais, as well as Apamea, their first stronghold, while Demetrius II held onto Seleucia Pieria and the Phoenician cities of Sidon and Tyre, and retained the loyalty of Babylonia.

Ill. 5.15. Demetrius II Theos Philadelphus Nicator (first reign, 146-138 BCE). AR tetradrachm (31 mm, 16.43 gm). Antioch mint. Diademed head of the young Demetrius II / Apollo seated on an omphalos, holding an arrow in his right hand and a bow in his left; monogram at the knee; a palm branch in the outer left field. The Greek inscription reads ΒΑΣΙΛΕΩΣ ΔΗΜΗΤΡΙΟΥ ΘΕΟΥ ΦΙΛΑΔΕΛΦΟΥ ΝΙΚΑΤΟΡΟΣ, "of King Demetrius *Theou Philadelpou Nikatoros* (the brother-loving god and the victorious)". In exergue, ΖΞΡ = SE 167 (146/5 BCE), and monogram. *SC* no. 1906.5d.

His adoption of the titles "god" and "the victorious" may be seen as manifestations of Demetrius' arrogance and vanity.

The epithet "Nicator" was adopted following Demetrius' defeat of Alexander *Balas*, while his title "Philadelphus" (brother-loving) memorialised his brother, Antigonus, who was killed when Alexander seized the throne (Livy, *Periochae* 50.4).

The Maccabees played on the ebb and flow of the struggle between the rivals for control of the Seleucid kingdom. Although they occasionally misjudged the intentions of the fractious Seleucid claimants and Jonathan made a grievous mistake in placing his trust in the treacherous Tryphon, which resulted in his murder in c. 142 BCE, they managed to win total autonomy for a period of about four years.

A similar development occurred in the east, where most spectacularly in 141 BCE the Parthians overran the province of Babylonia and took its capital, Seleucia-on-the-Tigris. Demetrius II responded with a military campaign against the Parthians, leaving Cleopatra behind in Seleucia Pieria. He managed to briefly recover Seleucia-on-the-Tigris, as evidenced by an issue of tetradrachms in his name there. However, the situation in Babylonia remained fluid and there was some unknown incident in which Demetrius was taken captive by the Parthians. For the next ten years he was detained at the pleasure of Arsacid king, Mithradates I, and obliged to reside at their royal court in Hyrcania on the shore of the Caspian Sea. Despite being accorded domestic comforts and a Parthian princess, Rhodogune, to keep him company, Demetrius was restless and twice tried to escape from his exile, once with the help of his friend Callimander, who had gone to great lengths to rescue the king: he had travelled incognito through Babylonia and Parthia. When the two friends were captured during their escape, the Parthian king did not punish Callimander but rewarded him for his fidelity to Demetrius. The second time that Demetrius tried to get away from Hyrcania, Mithradates humiliated him by giving him a golden set of dice, hinting that Demetrius II was a restless child who needed toys.

Ill. 5.16. Demetrius II Theos Philadelphus Nicator (first reign, 146-138 BCE). AR tetradrachm (27 mm, 13.76 gm). Sidon mint. Diademed and draped bust / Eagle standing with a palm frond behind; to the left, AOP date) = SE 171 = 142/1 BCE above a monogram; to the right, the mintmark ΣΙΔΩ (Sido[n]) above an aphlaston; control mark Γ between the legs. The Greek inscription reads ΒΑΣΙΛΕΩΣ ΔΗΜΗΤΡΙΟΥ, "of King Demetrius". *SC* no. 1954.5.

In an act of defiance to the new king, Jonathan and his supporters laid siege to the *Akra* fortress in Jerusalem, which held out as a symbol of residual Seleucid control over Judaea and a refuge for Jewish Hellenizers. Demetrius was greatly incensed when he heard about Jonathan's defiance. He appeared with an army at Ake-Ptolemais and demanded that Jonathan lift the siege of the *Akra*. Demetrius also summoned Jonathan to appear before him. Without raising the siege, Jonathan, accompanied by Jewish elders and priests, went to the king and mollified him with precious gifts. The upshot of their meeting was that the young king did not merely confirm him in his office of High Priest and honour him as one of his chief 'Friends', but gave to him the three Samarian districts of Aphairema (Mount Ephraim), Lydda (Lod), and Ramathaim, to the northwest of Judaea. No doubt realising Demetrius' susceptibility to bribery, Jonathan handed over to him 300 talents, receiving in return exemption from tribute for the whole of Judaea. These substantial concessions were confirmed in writing. Jonathan repeated his demand that the Seleucid garrison relinquish the Akra and, with Demetrius facing an insurrection by his troops, the Seleucid monarch assured him that this would duly happen, although he failed to fulfil this promise [1 Macc. 11.20-42].

With the spread of the rebellion to Antioch, Demetrius II appealed to Jonathan for military support. Jonathan dispatched 3,000 men to protected Demetrius in his capital against his own subjects [1 Macc. 11.44-53]. The Jewish fighters proceeded to slaughter the rebels and no doubt some innocent civilians, sacked the city and set it on fire on fire. The citizens instantly submitted to Demetrius and Jonathan's men were withdrawn to Judaea. Thereupon, Demetrius reneged on his promises to Jonathan and renewed his hostility.

Principal Ancient Sources:
1 Maccabees 10.67-14.3, 11.20-42, 44-53.
Appian, *Syriaca* 67-68.
Diodorus Siculus 32.9c-10.1; 33.4-4a.
Eusebius, *Chronicon* p.255.
Josephus, *Antiquitates Judaicae* (*AJ*) 13.109-186.
Justin, *Epitome* 35.2.
Livy, *Periochae* 50.4, 52.11.

Antiochus VI Epiphanes Dionysos (144 - c.142 BCE) [Grainger 1997, 28-29; *SC* 2.1, 315] was the infant son of Alexander *Balas* and Cleopatra Thea, who been in the fostering care and protection of an 'Arab' (probably Ituraean) clan chief following his father's death. Diodotus/Tryphon saw the advantage to him of rallying support against Demetrius by adopting the young Antiochus. His initial base was at Chalcis by Belus (present day Qinnasrîn in northern Syria), not far from Antioch. By 144 BCE his party had gained control of Apamea and within a year they had displaced Demetrius II from Antioch. The administration of Ake-Ptolemais rallied to the Banner of Antiochus soon afterwards as did Judaea and much of Coele-Syria, including the port cities of Sidon and Tyre. In about 142 BCE, Tryphon took the diadem for himself, after his young charge either died naturally or was murdered.

After Diodotus Tryphon and Antiochus VI seized the Seleucid capital, Antioch, Jonathan instantly switched his allegiance, especially as the latter confirmed all the privileges previously granted to him and appointed his brother Simon *strategos* (commander) of the sea coast, from the 'Ladder of Tyre' to the Egyptian frontier. Jonathan embarked on a tour of the coastal towns over which he had been given military command. He received a favourable reception in Ascalon, but Gaza was hostile and denied him entry. Jonathan blockaded the town and pillaged its exposed suburbs, causing its citizens to sue for peace. The terms they were given required

Ill. 5.17. Antiochus VI Epiphanes Dionysus (144-c.142 BCE). AR tetradrachm (32 mm, 15.39 gm). Antioch mint, 144/3 BCE. Diademed and radiate head of Antiochus VI / The Dioscuri riding; above and below, the Greek inscription reads ΒΑΣΙΛΕΩΣ ΑΝΤΙΟΧΟΥ ΕΠΙΦΑΝΟΥΣ ΔΙΟΝΥΣΟΥ, "of King Antiochus, *Epiphanes Dionysos* (manifest as Dionysus)"; to right, ΤΡΥ(ΦΩΝ) = Tryphon (his guardian). Immediately below the horses, the date, ΘΞΡ = SE 169 (144/3 BCE), and ΣΤΑ. A wreath of lilies and grain ears defines the border. *SC* no. 2000.2a.

The epithet "Epiphanes" evidently refers to Antiochus IV, whose grandson Antiochus VI was claimed to be. The rays on the portrait head are an expression of his deification as Dionysus incarnate (while Antiochus IV was presented as Zeus incarnate). The Dioscuri, archetypal heroes of Classical mythology, featuring on his tetradrachms, were a popular subject of that period, appearing regularly on the coins of Eucratides of Bactria and on contemporaneous Roman republican denarii.

Ill. 5.18. Antiochus VI Epiphanes Dionysus. AR drachms (19 mm, 4.02 gm; 17 mm, 4.05 gm, respectively). Antioch mint. Radiate and diademed head of Antiochus VI. The Greek inscription reads ΒΑΣΙΛΕΩΣ ΑΝΤΙΟΧΟΥ ΕΠΙΦΑΝΟΥΣ ΔΙΟΝΥΣΟΥ, "of King Antiochus *Epiphanes Dionysos*". (a) Apollo seated on an omphalos, holding an arrow in his right hand and a bow in his left; monogram between the legs. In exergue, ΟΡ = SE 170 (143/2 BCE), and ΣΤΑ. *SC* no. 2002.2d. (b) Undated issue, struck c. 142 BCE. Spiked Macedonian helmet with cheek guards, adorned with wild goat's horn above visor; ΤΡΥ above helmet, monogram to lower right. *SC* no. 2003e.

The change from (a) to (b) suggests that Tryphon's displacement of Antiochus VI was accomplished by a creeping takeover, rather than a sudden putsch. The dynastic Apollo type is replaced by Tryphon's favourite emblem, the Macedonian helmet with the wild goat's horn, the Seleucid era date is dispensed with and the abbreviated name ΣΤΑ is superseded by that of Tryphon (ΤΡΥ).

Ill. 5.19. Antiochus VI Epiphanes Dionysus. Æ tetrachalkon (20 mm, 7.72 gm). Apamea? mint. Radiate and diademed head of Antiochus VI ; incuse countermark, anchor / Panathenaic amphora; ΓΙ left, small palm right. The Greek inscription reads ΒΑΣΙΛΕΩΣ ΑΝΤΙΟΧΟΥ ΕΠΙΦΑΝΟΥΣ ΔΙΟΝΥΣΟΥ, "of King Antiochus *Epiphanes Dionysos*". *SC* no. 2015.1c.

The amphora for containing wine was often associated with the cult of Dionysus (such as found in the tomb paintings of c. 200 BCE at Marisa)

their magistrates to give up their sons as hostages, and they were sent to Jerusalem [1 Macc. 11.54-62].

While his brother Simon was left in Judaea to conquer Beth-zur, Jonathan headed north in the direction of Damascus. His troops were ambushed by an army of Demetrius II on the plain of Hazor, but then he managed to reverse the situation by inflicting a stunning defeat on the enemy at the same place. Buoyed up by this latest military success,

Jonathan now felt that he had achieved the stature of a regional power-broker. Accordingly, he dispatched a mission to Rome to renew the treaty of the Maccabees with the Roman Republic and exchanged friendly messages with Sparta and other states [1 Macc. 11.63-12.23]. However, the authenticity of some of the surviving documents in 1 Maccabees that refer to those diplomatic exchanges is contested.

Jonathan learnt that Demetrius' generals were determined to avenge the defeat inflicted on his forces at Hazor and had sent a larger force than before to oppose him. He sped north with his men to Hamath (Hama) in Syria to intercept the Seleucid army and pre-empt an attack on Judaea. Jonathan's spies reported that the opposing army was planning a night attack and he gave orders to his soldiers to remain on guard. On discovering that Jonathan and his men were remaining vigilant, the enemy lost heart and withdrew, but left their camp fires burning. By the time the Maccabaean fighters realised the deception played on them, it was too late to close in on the Seleucid army. Jonathan therefore gave the order to withdraw. Meanwhile, Simon and his supporters had seized Joppa (Iopé, Jaffa), thereby preventing its citizens from handing the town over to supporters of Demetrius. On Jonathan's return to Jerusalem, he convened the Jewish council (*hever*) and obtained its agreement to erect a number of fortresses in Judaea and rebuild the eastern wall of Jerusalem, which had partly collapsed into the Kedron ravine. It was also decided to build a high barrier to screen and isolate the *Akra* and its hostile garrison from Maccabaean-held Jerusalem [1 Macc. 12.24-38].

Hardly had the threat from Demetrius II been dealt with, then Tryphon and his partisans arrived at Beth-shean to challenge the Maccabees. In his usual fashion, Jonathan hastened towards Beth-shean with a large contingent of troops. Feeling intimidated by his opponent's strength, Tryphon changed his tune and endeavoured to conciliate Jonathan with honours and gifts. He cunningly persuaded Jonathan to dismiss most of his forces and accompany him to Ake-Ptolemais, which he promised to hand over to Jonathan along with many fortresses.

Jonathan fell into Tryphon's trap and proceeded to Ptolemais with just 1,000 of his men, all of whom were killed, while he himself was taken prisoner [1 Macc. 12.24-53]. Although Tryphon also attempted to wipe out the residual 3,000 Maccabaean troops stationed in Galilee, through their tight discipline and bravery, they were able to beat a successful retreat to Judaea [1 Macc. 12.30-52].

Simon *Thassi* was acclaimed leader of the Judaeans in place of his captive brother. He lost no time in mustering forces and completing Jerusalem's defences. Predictably, Tryphon and his army, with his prisoner Jonathan in tow, left Ake-Ptolemais and headed towards Judaea. He encountered Simon's forces encamped at Adida (Hadid) who were ready to join him in battle. Tryphon sent envoys to Simon with demands for a ransom of 100 talents and Jonathan's two sons as hostages, in return for which he promised to release his captive. Although Simon did not trust Tryphon, he complied with the request in order that he might not be accused of contributing to the death of his brother. But Tryphon did not liberate his prisoner. Simon blocked his progress through Judaea and a snowstorm prevented Tryphon from relieving the *Akra* from the direction of the Judaean wilderness to the east. Thus thwarted, he withdrew east of the Jordan to Gilead and executed Jonathan at Baskama in 143 BCE [1 Macc. 13.12-24]. Nothing further is known of the two captive sons of Jonathan. One of his daughters was the ancestress of the historian, Josephus [*Vita* 1].

Principal Ancient Sources:
1 Maccabees 11.39-13.32.
Appian, *Syriaca* 68.
Diodorus Siculus 32.9d-10; 33.4a, 28, 28a.
Josephus, *Bellum Judaicum* (*BJ*) 1.48-49.
Josephus, *Antiquitates Judaicae* (*AJ*) 13.131-132, 144-153, 187, 218-219.
Josephus, *Vita* 1.
Justin, *Epitome* 36.1.
Livy, *Periochae* 52.13; 55.11.

(Diodotus) Tryphon Autocrator (c.142-138 BCE) [Grainger 1997, 69-70; *SC* 2.1. 335-36] duly assumed the royal title for himself, and adopted the name "Tryphon", literally "the one who represents magnificence". In c.142 BCE, Tryphon announced the death of Antiochus VI, claiming that his young charge had contracted an illness and supposedly required surgery, during which he died – possibly as a cover for his murder. He sent an envoy to Babylon early in 140 BCE, apparently to seek recognition of his kingship, but to no avail. He also attempted to humour the Roman Senate with the gift of a precious gold statue of a winged Victory, with the weight of 10,000 gold staters, i.e. about 100 kg of gold. It was accepted without qualms, but then the Senate decreed that the name of the king who had been treacherously murdered be engraved on it and not that of the wicked perpetrator [Diodorus Siculus, 33.28a].

Tryphon again manifested his treachery in the way he lured the Jewish leader and High Priest, Jonathan *Apphus,* to his death. In one respect, though, he was quite frank. Tryphon did not feign a blood relationship with the Seleucid royal house, styling himself baldly as *Autokrator* ("self-empowered") on his coins.

At its largest extent, Tryphon's realm included Antioch, Apamea and much of northern Syria, Byblus in northern Phoenicia and most of Coele-Syria but not Gaza.

In the autumn of 138 BCE, Antiochus VII *Sidetes*, the younger brother of Demetrius II, landed with a sizeable force at Seleucia Pieria to claim his inheritance. He rapidly gained possession of northern Syria and then rolled back Tryphon and his supporters southwards along the coast of Phoenicia, pinning the usurper down for a time at Dora. Tryphon managed to slip through the siege of Dora and rushed north to Apamea, where he was cornered and killed (in late 138 BCE or in early 137 BCE).

Simon (surnamed *Thassi*, of uncertain meaning) the last of the sons of Mattathias, became the next High Priest in addition to his assumed role of commander of the Jewish forces (ruling from 142 to 135 BCE). The Hasmonaean dynasty was established by a resolution adopted at a large assembly called in 140 BCE "of the priests, people, rulers of the nation, and elders of the land", confirming "Simon as their leader and High Priest in perpetuity, until a true prophet should appear" [1 Macc. 14.41]. Recognition of the new dynasty by the Senate of the Roman Republic was accorded at about the same time [1 Macc. 14.24].

Having broken with Tryphon, Simon made his peace with Demetrius II. At this point it appears that he effectively managed to break free of Seleucid tutelage, taking advantage of the open warfare that raged between rival Seleucid kings. This situation lasted for about four years to 138 BCE, more or less coinciding with the reign of Tryphon. One of Simon's first moves was to seize two

Ill. 5.20. (Diodotus) Tryphon Autocrator (c.142-138 BCE). AR drachm (33 mm, 16.99 gm). Antioch mint. Diademed head of Tryphon / Spiked Macedonian helmet, adorned with wild goat's (ibex's) horn above visor (perhaps representing the horn of the goat Amalthea who suckled the infant Zeus), thunderbolt of Zeus on the cheek-pieces and diadem hanging from the brim; ΠΑ monogram to the inner left, all within oak wreath border. The Greek inscription reads ΒΑΣΙΛΕΩΣ ΤΡΥΦΩΝΟΣ [Α]ΥΤΟΚΡΑΤΟΡΟΣ, "of King Tryphon, *Autokrator* (self-empowered)". *SC* no. 2031.1. Roma Numismatics Auction 7 (22 March 2014), lot 827; courtesy Roma Numismatics Ltd.

This highly distinctive helmet, which is likely to have some cultic as well as military significance, is closely associated with Tryphon because it is found exclusively on his coins and some issues of his ward, Antiochus VI.

Ill. 5.21. (Diodotus) Tryphon Autocrator. Æ tetrachalkon (16 mm, 7.8 gm). Antioch mint. Diademed head of Tryphon / Spiked Macedonian helmet, similar to that in Ill. 5.20; with a starburst to the left. *SC* no. 2034e.

important fortified positions, the town of Gazara and the *Akra* fortress in Jerusalem. These two objectives were successfully accomplished in 141 BCE [1 Macc. 13.43-52].

Simon's rule of Judaea was characterised by relative peace and prosperity [1 Macc. 14.8-13]. Tryphon had little to show for his stratagems targeting Judaea other than a relatively modest one-off tribute of 100 talents of silver [1 Macc. 13.16]. It must have been during this time of nominal independence that Simon commenced the construction of a monumental family mausoleum at Modi'in, situated about 30 km northwest of Jerusalem, to which he brought the body of his brother Jonathan [Macc. 13.25-30].

The increasing diplomatic intercourse with the Seleucids and other Mediterranean powers resulted in the Hasmonaean ruling élite adopting many of the typical trappings of Hellenistic monarchy. The dynastic mausoleum at Modi'in was a resplendent Hellenistic monument. Simon permitted his subjects to set up bronze tablets on a monument on Mount Zion and in the Temple precincts, bearing an honorific inscription in typical Greek fashion [1 Macc. 14.27-49]. Simon's son, John *Hyrcanus* I began a trend of giving popular Macedonian-Greek names to his sons (Aristobulus, Antigonus, Alexander), while Alexander Jannaeus adopted the royal title, *basileus*, which figures

> in the Greek inscriptions on his coins. Hyrcanus created the precedent for the Hasmonaeans of employing foreign mercenaries, a common practice of Hellenistic kings [Josephus, *BJ* 1.61; *AJ* 13.249].

Principal Ancient Sources:
1 Maccabees 11.39-40, 54-56; 12.41-53; 13.12-52; 14.1-3, 8-13, 24, 27-52; 15.10-14, 25, 37.
Appian, *Syriaca* 11.68.
Diodorus Siculus, 32.9c; 33.3, 4a, 28-28a.
Josephus, *Bellum Judaicum* (*BJ*) 1.50-51, 61.
Josephus, *Antiquitates Judaicae* (*AJ*) 13.131-132, 144, 184-187, 203-209, 218-224, 249.
Justin, *Epitome* 36.1; 38.9.
Livy, *Periochae* 52.13; 55.11.
Strabo, *Geographia* 14.5.2; 16.2.10.

THE MILITARY CHARACTER OF THE MACCABAEAN STATE

Military achievement was one of the defining characteristics of the Hasmonaean dynasty during its ascendancy in the generations of the Maccabees and their immediate successors [Jacobson 2013b]. From the description of the dynastic mausoleum of the Maccabees at Modi'in, their most celebrated monument, we learn that the main theme of its decorative scheme was a celebration of arms:

> "Simon built a high monument over the tomb of his father and his brothers, visible at a great distance, faced back and front with polished stone. He erected seven pyramids, those for his father and mother and his four brothers arranged in pairs. For the pyramids he contrived an elaborate setting; he surrounded them with great columns surmounted with trophies of armour for a perpetual memorial, and between the trophies carved ships, plainly visible to all at sea. This mausoleum which he made at Modein stands to this day" [1 Macc. 13.27-30].

> "And Simon also built for his father and brothers a very great monument of polished white marble, and raising it to a great and conspicuous height, made porticoes round it, and erected monolithic pillars, a wonderful thing to see. In addition to these he built for his parents and his brothers seven pyramids, one for each, so made as to excite wonder by their size and beauty; and these have been preserved to this day" [Josephus, *AJ* 13.211-12].

The form of this sculptural composition may be deduced from contemporaneous architectural decoration that has survived in monuments in Asia Minor, such as the sanctuary of Athena Polias in Pergamon.

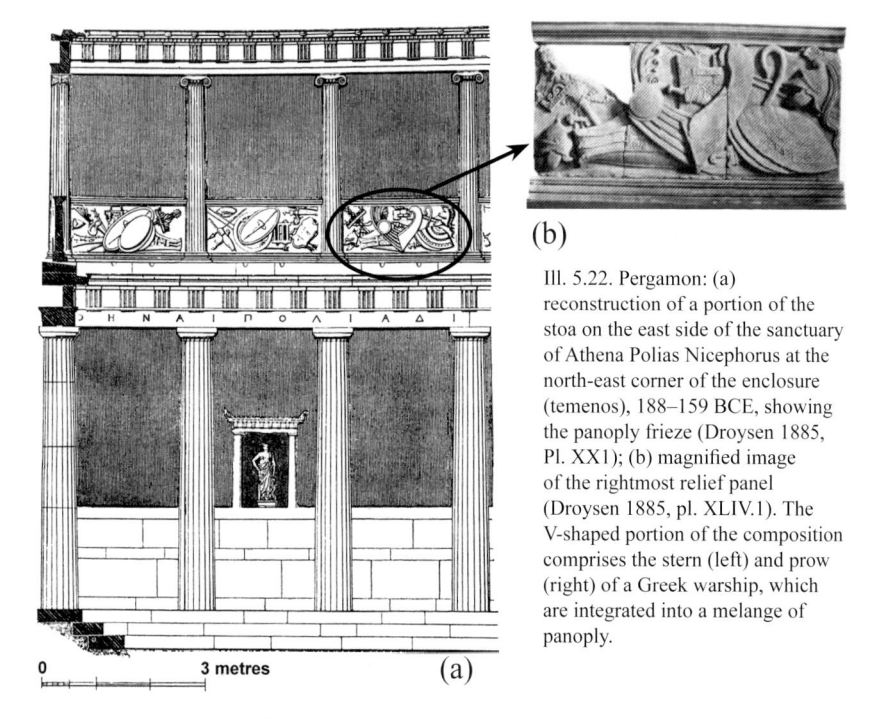

Ill. 5.22. Pergamon: (a) reconstruction of a portion of the stoa on the east side of the sanctuary of Athena Polias Nicephorus at the north-east corner of the enclosure (temenos), 188–159 BCE, showing the panoply frieze (Droysen 1885, Pl. XX1); (b) magnified image of the rightmost relief panel (Droysen 1885, pl. XLIV.1). The V-shaped portion of the composition comprises the stern (left) and prow (right) of a Greek warship, which are integrated into a melange of panoply.

From the description of this mausoleum in 1 Maccabees, we learn that it possessed a peripteral colonnade carrying a frieze decorated with a martial composition of armour, alternating with (war) ships. The panoply friezes above porticos fringing the enclosure of the temple of Athena Polias Nicephorus at Pergamon, dating from the reign of Eumenes II (188-159 BCE), include portions of warships intermixed with helmets and other items of armour and weaponry, which evidently reflects the type of decoration that graced the Maccabaean mausoleum . There can be little doubt that it was deliberately chosen to celebrate the military achievements of the Maccabees and therefore the funerary monument was also a *tropaeum* or victory memorial.

The two documentary accounts of the monument inform us that the Maccabaean mausoleum was topped by six pyramids arranged in pairs, as cenotaphs for the founder of the dynasty, Mattathias, together with his wife and four illustrious sons, Judah, Eleazar, Jonathan and John (Yehoḥanan). The seventh pyramid, which may have been erected in the middle of the ensemble, would have been intended to commemorate Simon *Thassi*, the builder of the sepulchral monument. The arrangement of six cenotaphs in three ordered pairs was also used for the tombs of the Patriarchs in Hebron, which correspond to those commemorating Abraham and Sarah, Isaac and Rebecca and Jacob and Leah. This latter monument, as constructed by Herod the Great in the late 1st century BCE survives largely intact with its ordered arrangement of patriarchal cenotaphs.

Ill. 5.23. Herodian Enclosure of the Tombs of the Patriarchs (Haram al-Khalil), Hebron, late 1st century BCE
http://en.wikipedia.org/wiki/Cave_of_the_Patriarchs#mediaviewer/File:Israel_Hebron_Cave_of_the_Patriarchs.jpg. Courtesy of Wikipedia and Creative Commons Org.

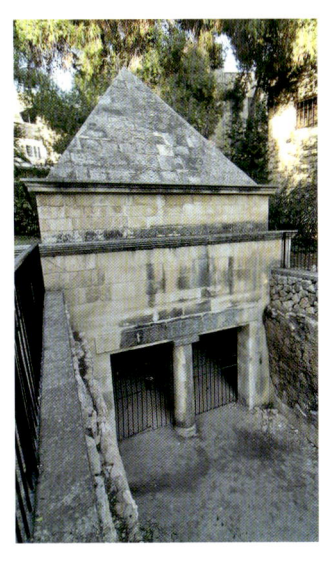

Ill. 5.24. The Tomb of Jason in the Rehavia neighbourhood to the west of the Old City of Jerusalem, which is believed to date from the reign of Alexander Jannaeus (103-76 BCE), on the basis of the pottery and coins that were found there. Its design, featuring a pyramidal roof capping a cube and colonnaded facade, is modelled on an arrangement that was much favoured in east Greek lands, exemplified by the famous Mausoleum of Halicarnassus, one of the Wonders of the Ancient World. Photograph courtesy of Professor Shimon Gibson.

Funerary monuments topped with pyramids enjoyed much favour in east Greek lands, including Judaea in the Hellenistic period, taking as their model the famous Mausoleum of Halicarnassus, one of the Wonders of the Ancient World. An early example in Jerusalem is Jason's tomb, which appears to date from the early 1st century BCE.

Military motifs also feature on the earliest issues of Hasmonaean coinage, struck by John *Hyrcanus* I (135-104 BCE), the son and successor of Simon *Thassi*. These include a crested helmet on his largest coin (dichalkon), a wreath on the chalkon denomination and a palm branch with a ribbon, or fillet band, tied to the tip of the branch on the hemichalkon issued by Hyrcanus (see below). This filleted palm branch is a well-recognised Greek victory symbol with both divine and royal connotations, which was already encountered on one of the two representative tetradrachms of Seleucus IV, illustrated earlier. We are told that palm branches, probably tied with ribbons, were carried in the victory procession following the fall of the *Akra* fortress to Simon and his followers [1 Macc. 13.52].

WHERE IS THE MACCABAEAN MAUSOLEUM?

In the 4th century CE, the village of Modein still existed, according to the Bishop of Caesarea and early Christian author, Eusebius (*Onomasticon* 132.16), and the tombs of the Maccabees were pointed out there, although it is not certain that the monumental mausoleum remained. The site is marked on the famous 6th century Byzantine mosaic map of the Holy Land on a floor of a church in Madaba (Medeba) in Jordan, accompanied by the following caption: "Modeim, today Moditha, from here were the Maccabeans".

Modein has been identified with Khirbet al-Midya, in the foothills to the east of Lod, since 1866, largely on their similar sounding names (a criterion that has proved effective in identifying many ancient sites), and the area has been subject to archaeological investigations from that time, but no positive evidence has yet been found of the Maccabaean mausoleum. The rock-cut tombs that are popularly pointed out as the 'Tombs of the Maccabees' are of Byzantine date and therefore have no connection with the ancient Jewish heroes. More recently, Shimon Gibson has suggested Givat Titura, on high ground a few miles to the east of Khirbet al-Midya as the likely site of the mausoleum. There are fairly abundant archaeological remains there from the Late Hellenistic and Early Roman Periods (late 2nd century BCE to the early 2nd century CE), but the ongoing search for the Maccabaean mausoleum is proving somewhat elusive.

CHAPTER 6.

FROM ANTIOCHUS VII TO ANTIOCHUS IX – CONSOLIDATION OF HASMONAEAN RULE

BCE) [Grainger 1997, 29-31; *SC* 2.1, 349-50], nicknamed **Sidetes** (from Side in Pamphylia, where he spent his early years out of harm's way), made a bid for the Seleucid throne after learning of the capture of his elder brother, Demetrius II. On arrival at Seleucia Pieria in 138 BCE, the refuge of Queen Cleopatra Thea, Antiochus and his troops were admitted to her stronghold. Believing that Demetrius would not return, Antiochus married Cleopatra, who was about five years older than him. She was to bear him five children, three sons, including a future king – Antiochus IX – and two daughters.

After the demise of Tryphon, Antiochus ruled without an internal rival and was the last Seleucid ruler over a unified kingdom. This emboldened him to repudiate earlier agreements that made concessions to Maccabaean-ruled Judaea. He demanded subservience from Judaea and the return of all towns that the Maccabees had occupied, even those within Judaea proper, including Iopé (Jaffa) and Gazara (Gezer) as well as the handing back of the *Akra* fortress in Jerusalem, conditions that Simon *Thassi* explained to Athenobius, an envoy of

Ill. 6.1. Antiochus VII Euergetes *Sidetes* (138-129 BCE). AR tetradrachm (30 mm, 16.46 gm). Antioch mint. Diademed head of Antiochus VII / Athena standing half-left, holding a Nike in her right hand, shield and spear in her left; monogram and A to the left; all within an olive wreath border. The Greek inscription reads ΒΑΣΙΛΕΩΣ ΑΝΤΙΟΧΟΥ ΕΥΕΡΓΕΤΟΥ, "of King Antiochus *Euergetes* (benefactor)". *SC* no. 2061.3a.

The epithet "Euergetes" has some justification. The reign of Antiochus VII was relatively stable and not rent by dynastic strife. Moreover, he acquired a reputation for graciousness and kindness. For example, when Jerusalem was being besieged by his army, he granted a truce during the festival of Tabernacles and, as a generous and respectful gesture to the Jews, presented bulls for whole-offerings in the Temple [Josephus, *AJ* 13.242-244; Plutarch, *Moralia* (*Regum et Imperatorum apophthegmata*) 184E-F]. A gold stater of Antiochus VII adds the epithet "Megas (the Great)" to his other title, which is also attested by two honorific inscriptions from Delos [*SC* 2, 354]. The featuring of Athena possibly refers to the cult of that goddess that was prominent at Side, Antiochus' birthplace.

Ill. 6.2. Antiochos VII Sidetes. Æ hemichalkon or chalkon (12mm; 1.47 gm). Iopé (Jaffa) mint (?). Crested Boeotian helmet with cheek guards / aphlaston. The Greek inscription reads ΒΑΣΙΛΕ[ΩΣ A]NTIOXOY, "of King Antiochus". SC 2122.

The military types (helmet and aphlaston) point to this issue being connected with Antiochus' campaign against Tryphon at the start of his reign, and a military mint, possibly on the move with the army of the former along the Phoenician coast, in pursuit of Tryphon's forces. That contest preoccupied Antiochus' attention at that time, preventing him from confronting Simon and his Hasmonaean followers. The crested helmet on this coin probably constituted the prototype for the helmet on the dichalkon of John *Hyrcanus* I (see Ill. 6.11). The aphlaston would suit a maritime location in the southern Levant.

Antiochus, were unacceptable [1 Macc. 15.26-36]. Shortly afterwards, Simon was murdered by his son-in-law, and it was left to his surviving son, John *Hyrcanus*, to bear the brunt of Antiochus' aggression. The Seleucid king led an army to attack Judaea and lay siege to Jerusalem in 135/4 BCE. Before agreeing to lift the siege, he made *Hyrcanus* agree to recognise him as Judaea's sovereign, hand over the arms of his men and pay tribute to him for keeping the towns near Judaea's borders [Josephus, *AJ* 13.236-249; Diodorus Siculus, 34/35.1]. *Hyrcanus* successfully resisted Antiochus' demand to place a Seleucid garrison in Jerusalem.

Antiochus VII's attention was then diverted to dangers looming in the east that threatened the integrity of his kingdom. Osrhoene, with its capital at Edessa on the upper Euphrates split away from the Seleucid kingdom and transferred its allegiance to the Parthians. In 130 BCE, Antiochus undertook a large expedition to the east, which included contingents conscripted from Judaea, led by John *Hyrcanus*, and also contingents drawn from other autonomous states that had formerly belonged to the Seleucid realm. His campaign began well, winning battles and he succeeded in occupying Seleucia on the Tigris and Babylon. He then proceeded to Media. In the spring of 129 BCE, he offered the Parthian king, Phraates II, a peace treaty, if he would withdraw his army to his ancestral territory and pay tribute, terms that were quite similar to those that he had pressed on John *Hyrcanus* earlier. These terms were rejected and Phraates released Demetrius II from captivity, with the intention of creating mayhem

(a)

(b)

among the Seleucids. In the autumn of that year, the Parthians attacked the Seleucid expeditionary force and Antiochus was killed in the fighting. His body was allowed to be brought back to Antioch for burial, but the two royal children who had accompanied Antiochus were taken to the Parthian court, where they remained. This battle was a watershed, marking the permanent loss of all Seleucid territories east of Syria. Meanwhile, Demetrius II managed to reach Antioch safely, despite an attempt by Phraates to recapture him, and he regained both throne and queen.

The Seleucid kingdom was now but a shadow of its former self, with multiple claimants contesting control of the rump of the realm in almost continuous civil war. Amid this turmoil, Judaea was able to enjoy *de facto* independence, with John *Hyrcanus* I proclaiming his sovereignty by striking bronze coins in his own name.

Ill. 6.3. Issue struck by John *Hyrcanus* I for Antiochus VII *Sidetes*. Æ prutah/ chalkon (15 mm, 2.9 gm and 15 mm, 2.6 gm, respectively). Jerusalem mint. Lily (*candidum*) / Inverted anchor (emblem of the Seleucid monarchy). The complete Greek inscription to the left and right of the anchor reads ΒΑΣΙΛΕΩΣ ΑΝΤΙΟΧΟΥ ΕΥΕΡΓΕΤΟΥ, "of King Antiochus Euergetes". In exergue, (a) ***above***: ΑΠΡ = SE 181 (132/1 BCE); *SC* no. 2123.1; (b) ***below***: ΒΠΡ = SE 182 (131/0 BCE); *SC* no. 2123.2; see *TJC*, 30-31.

This issue attests to the submission of John *Hyrcanus* I as a vassal of Antiochus VII. The lily was a regular Jewish symbol in antiquity and featured in the decoration of the Temple in Jerusalem and on the vestments of the High Priest [Jacobson 2013a, 16-17]

On the eve of his return to Syria to regain the Seleucid throne in 138 BCE, Antiochus *Sidetes* wrote to Simon, informing him of his plans. He assured Simon that he recognised the gains achieved by the Maccabees, including exemption from tribute, right to maintain an army and possession of fortifications. Moreover, according to 1 Maccabees, Antiochus granted Simon the right to mint his own coinage, although this concession was not acted on [1 Macc. 15.1-9].

When *Sidetes* cornered Tryphon at Dor, Simon was prepared to assist him with troops, equipment and bullion, but was rebuffed. Having achieved success, Antiochus VII *Sidetes* reneged on his promises and demanded the return to Seleucid control of all cities that the Maccabees had captured, the restoration of a Seleucid garrison to the *Akra* in Jerusalem and the payment of a large indemnity. He threatened a renewal of hostilities should Simon fail to comply. One of *Sidetes'* courtiers, a certain Athenobius, visited Jerusalem and his report of the splendour of Simon's court and his wealth raised tensions to breaking point. Judaea was invaded by a Seleucid army under Kendebaeus, who had been given military responsibility over the coastal area of the southern Levant. Simon appointed his sons John and Judah to lead the campaign against Kendebaeus, with a sizeable force of infantry and cavalry. The Seleucid army was joined in battle in the plain below Modi'in and routed by John and Judah, although the latter was wounded in the encounter. The remnants of Kendebaeus' army sought refuge in Azotus (Ashdod), but John attacked them there and set fire to the town [1 Macc. 15.25-16.10].

In February 135 BCE, Simon, along with his two older sons, Mattathias and Judah, were invited to a banquet at the fortress of Dok, overlooking Jericho, by his son-in-law Ptolemy, son of Abubus. Ptolemy, who had gained power and wealth through his relationship with Simon, had hatched a plot to remove Simon and his sons and take power for himself. At the banquet, the guests were lavishly entertained and encouraged to drink their fill. Then they were sprung upon by hired assassins and treacherously murdered. Simon was succeeded by his third son, John *Hyrcanus* I, who was in Gazara (Gezer) at the time. John ruled as *Ethnarch* (= leader of his nation) and High Priest from 135-104 BCE. Having firmly established his authority in Syria, *Sidetes* demanded recognition of his authority in Judaea. When the Jews failed to accede to his demands, he resorted to force, laying siege to Jerusalem in 135 BCE. According to Josephus, the Hasmonaean king John *Hyrcanus* opened King David's sepulchre and removed three thousand talents, most of which he made over to Antiochus to spare the city. Famine forced John *Hyrcanus* to seek terms with *Sidetes*. In the Autumn of 134 BCE Antiochus VII granted peace with some strings attached, including a demand that the Jews acknowledge him as their sovereign and he also insisted on the dismantling of Jerusalem's fortifications [1 Macc. 16.11-24; Josephus, *BJ* 1.54-61; *AJ* 13.228-253].

Principal Ancient Sources:
1 Maccabees 15-16.10.
Appian, *Syriaca* 68.
Athenaeus, 153A;210C-D; 439D-E; 540B-C.
Diodorus Siculus, 34/35.1, 15-18.
Eusebius, *Chronicon* p.255-258.
Josephus, *Bellum Judaicum* (*BJ*) 1.50-51, 54-62
Josephus, *Antiquitates Judaicae* (*AJ*) 7.393, 13.219-253.
Josephus, *Contra Apionem* (*CA*) 2.82.
Justin, *Epitome* 38.9-10; 39.1.
Livy, *Periochae* 57.8; 59.13.
Plutarch, *Moralia* (*Regum et Imperatorum apophthegmata*) 184D-F.
Strabo, *Geographia* 14.5.2.

Demetrius II Theos Nicator (second reign, 129 – 126/5 BCE) [Grainger 1997, 43-44; *SC* 2.1, 409], once restored to the Seleucid throne, his authority was widely recognised throughout the Seleucid realm.

Not long after his return, he became involved in internal strife that was then plaguing the Ptolemaic royal house. He responded to an appeal from his mother-in-law, Cleopatra II Philometor, to support her against her brother and former husband, Ptolemy VIII Euergetes II (*Physcon*). Demetrius and his army encountered Ptolemy *Physcon* at Pelusium in the spring of 128 BCE, but broke off the engagement with his forces, after a revolt broke out in Syria, fomented by Ptolemy who also put forward a new Seleucid pretender, Alexander *Zabinas*.

Recollections of his cruelties and vices made him deeply unpopular. In 125 BCE, he sustained a heavy defeat at the hands of Alexander *Zabinas* near Damascus. He fled to Ake-Ptolemais, only to find that his wife Cleopatra Thea had shut the city gates before him. Then he sped to Tyre, where he met his death at the hands of the townspeople.

> During his second reign, Demetrius sought an opportunity to cross swords with *Hyrcanus*, who was reasserting the independence of Judaea after the death of Antiochus VII. However, having simultaneously to contend with *Zabinas* and expend efforts in trying to impose his authority in Syria, he found neither the time nor occasion to act on this intention [Josephus, *AJ* 13.267]. *Hyrcanus* took advantage of waning Seleucid authority to terminate Hasmonaean allegiance and with it tribute and military support. At the same time, he was able to expand his domain and increase his power and wealth [Josephus, *AJ* 13.273].

Ill. 6.4. Demetrius II Theos Nicator (second reign, 129-126/5 BCE). AR tetradrachms (29 mm, 16.80 gm and 33 mm, 14.06 gm respectively). (a) *Above*: Diademed head of Demetrius II with a beard / Zeus seated, holding a Nike with a wreath in his right hand and sceptre in his left; monogram below the throne. Antioch mint. AP below the throne; to the left, Ξ; the Greek inscription reads ΒΑΣΙΛΕΩΣ ΔΗΜΗΤΡΙΟΥ ΘΕΟΥ ΝΙΚΑΤΟΡΟΣ, "of King Demetrius *Theos Nikator* (victorious god)". *SC* no. 2166.2e.

The portrayal of Demetrius II with a beard on many of the coins of his second reign shows that he adopted some Parthian lifestyle habits during his years of captivity, including the wearing of a beard. The reverse type of Zeus holding a winged Victory was appropriated from the coin types of Antiochus IV and his descendants, who Demetrius displaced.

(b) *Below*: Tyre mint. Diademed and draped bust / Eagle standing on prow, palm frond behind; to the left, a club surmounted by the Tyre monogram with a further monogram above; to right, a monogram above ΔΠΡ = SE 184 (129/8 BCE); an additional monogram between the legs; the Greek inscription reads ΒΑΣΙΛΕΩΣ ΔΗΜΗΤΡΙΟΥ, of King Demetrius. *SC* no. 2195.2b. The head of Demetrius II on coins struck at Tyre during his second reign depict the king as clean-shaven, in contrast with coin portraits from other mints.

The epithet "Philadelphus (brother-loving)" which Demetrius II had included during his first reign was omitted during his second reign, probably because the early death of his brother Antigonus was judged to be no longer relevant and, besides, his release from Parthian detention by Phraates II, with the intention of undermining the eastern campaign of his younger brother, Antiochus VII, would have sorely tested the sincerity of such a proclaimed virtue.

90   ANTIOCH AND JERUSALEM

Principal Ancient Sources:
Appian, *Syriaca* 68.
Eusebius, *Chronicon* pp.257-258.
Josephus, *Antiquitates Judaicae* 13.254-265, 267-268, 273.
Justin, *Epitome* 38.9-10; Prologus 39; 39.1.
Livy, *Periochae* 60.11.

Alexander II *Zabinas* (128-122 BCE) [Grainger 1997, 7; *SC* 2.1, 441] appears to have been the son of a Greek merchant in Egypt called Protarchus. *Zabinas* is a derogative nickname meaning 'the bought one.' In his bid for the Seleucid throne, he was presented as either an adopted son of Antiochus VII *Sidetes* or the natural son of Alexander I *Balas* (see below). He won over the populace of Antioch through his staging of a solemn funeral for Antiochus VII, whose body had been returned by the Parthians.

Alexander *Zabinas*' popularity was greatest in northern Syria. He had a genial manner and "made friends with *Hyrcanus*" [Josephus, *Antiquitates Judaicae* 13.269], recognising Judaean independence and turning a blind eye to its expansion under John *Hyrcanus*. During his rule, Ake-Ptolemais and the surrounding area remained in the possession of Cleopatra Thea. Otherwise, Alexander's rule over the rump of the Seleucid kingdom appeared to be secure, that is until reconciliation within

Ill. 6.5. Alexander II *Zabinas* (128-122 BCE). AR tetradrachms (30 mm, 16.43 gm and 29 mm, 16.48 gm, respectively). Diademed head of Alexander II / Zeus seated, holding a sceptre in his left hand and a winged Nike alighting from his outstretched right hand; monogram in the outer left field. The Greek inscription reads ΒΑΣΙΛΕΩΣ ΑΛΕΞΑΝΔΡΟΥ, "of King Alexander". The deployment of the seated Zeus type on the reverse is a token of affirmation of Alexander II's descent from Antiochus IV through Alexander I *Balas*. (a) ***Above***: Antioch mint. *SC* no. 2219.2e. (b) ***Below***: Damascus mint; in exergue, ΘΠΡ = SE 189 (124/3 BCE). *SC* no. 2248.5b.

the Ptolemaic monarchy resulted in Ptolemy VIII *Physcon* switching his support to his relative, Cleopatra Thea and her son Antiochus VIII *Gryphus*. In 122 BCE, *Gryphus* defeated *Zabinas*. The latter retreated to Antioch, where he violated the temple of Zeus, making off with the golden Nike from the outstretched hand of the precious cult statue, in order to pay his remaining troops with the proceeds. He is reported to have justified his act of sacrilege with the succinct comment "Zeus has given me Victory" [Justin 39.2.5]. The Nike on his tetradrachms is shown flying off from the right hand of Zeus, so that the anecdote reported by Justin may actually have its roots in this iconographic image. In this regard, the earlier source, Diodorus Siculus [34/35.28.1] merely states that *Zabinas* and his accomplices plundered the temple of Zeus. Whatever the truth, he was obliged to escape the fury of the Antiochenes and sought refuge in Seleucia Pieria but was repulsed. He fell into the hands of pirates who surrendered him to Antiochus Gryphus. Alexander *Zabinas* was either executed or forced to commit suicide.

Alexander *Zabinas* was the only late Seleucid not to widely use epithets on his coins. However, on a unique gold stater in the British Museum, ΘΕΟΥ ΕΠΙΦΑΝΟΥΣ ΝΙΚΗΦΟΡΟΥ (*"Theou Epiphanous Nikephorou*, (of) god made manifest, the victorious") appears, as on the coins of Antiochus IV. This evidently reflects his claim to have been a natural son of Alexander I (who in turn insisted that he was the son of Antiochus IV Epiphanes), as reported in Eusebius, after Porphyry [*Chronicon* 1.257]. A few types among his bronze coins employ an abbreviated form of these epithets (the word ΘΕΟΥ is omitted).

Principal Ancient Sources:
Diodorus Siculus, 34/35.22, 28.
Eusebius, *Chronicon* pp.257-258.
Josephus, *Antiquitates Judaicae* (*AJ*) 13.254-65, 267-269.
Justin, *Periochae* Prologus 39; 39.1-2.

Antiochus VIII Epiphanes *Gryphus* and Cleopatra Thea (joint rule, 125-121 BCE) [Grainger 1997, 31-32, 45-47; *SC* 2.1, 469], Coins struck for Cleopatra alone reveal that after the death of Demetrius II, she ruled on her own briefly, although her authority was evidently limited to Ake-Ptolemais. Her full title, "Thea Euteria (Goddess of the fruitful season)", appears on the tetradrachms issued in Ake-Ptolemais during her short sole reign, which implies that she received worship as a fertility goddess, a common aspect of the royal cult practiced in Ptolemaic Egypt.

Cleopatra's elder son by Demetrius, Seleucus (V), is reported to have been eliminated when he had made an attempt to take the royal diadem. After his death, the younger son of Demetrius II, Antiochus (VIII), was recalled by his mother from Athens, where he had been sent for his education. By 125 BCE mother and son had secured power in Antioch and were ruling jointly. Antiochus' prominent hook-nose (hence his Greek nickname, *Gryphus*) was an inherited feature that he passed on to his children.

Son of one Ptolemaic princess, Antiochus VIII married another in 124/3 BCE, Cleopatra Tryphaena (daughter of Ptolemy VIII *Physcon*), in accordance with Ptolemy's reconciliation with his niece, Cleopatra Thea, and abandonment of Alexander Zabinas. Antiochus VIII grew less compliant to his mother and, true to type, she responded by attempting to eliminate him. We are told that when he returned from a hunt one day, Cleopatra Thea offered Antiochus a cup of wine. He became suspicious and forced her to drink the wine, which killed her. Numismatic evidence suggests that she died in the autumn of 121 BCE.

Principal Ancient Sources:
Appian, *Syriaca* 69.
Eusebius, *Chronicon* pp.257-258.
Justin, *Epitome* 39.1-2.
Livy, *Periochae* 60.11.

Patronage of Athens during the Reigns of Antiochus VII and VIII

Antiochus IV had established a reputation as one of Athens' greatest benefactors which later Seleucid kings tried to emulate as far as they could. The cordial relations between the Seleucids and Athens, the hub of Hellenic culture and religion, seem to

Ill. 6.6. Cleopatra Thea and Antiochus VIII Epiphanes Philometor *Gryphus*, joint rule (125-121 BCE). AR tetradrachms (30 mm, 15.88 gm and 30 mm, 15.98 gm, respectively). Veiled head of Cleopatra Thea and diademed head of Antiochus VIII / Zeus seated, holding a Nike with a wreath in his right hand and a sceptre in his left; monogram in the outer left field. The Greek inscription reads ΒΑΣΙΛΙΣΣΗΣ ΚΛΕΟΠΑΤΡΑΣ ΘΕΑΣ ΚΑΙ ΒΑΣΙΛΕΩΣ ΑΝΤΙΟΧΟΥ, "of Queen Cleopatra *Thea* (goddess) and King Antiochus". (a) ***Above***: Ake-Ptolemais mint, *SC* no. 2271.1. (b) ***Below***: Damascus mint; in exergue, ΒϘΡ = SE 192 (121/120 BCE) repeated monogram below the seat of the throne. *SC* no. 2267.2a.

As these tetradrachms from the period of joint rule demonstrate, Cleopatra Thea had the upper hand. She is named as queen before Antiochus, her portrait is placed in front of his and is honoured with an epithet (*Thea*), while Antiochus is not.

Ill. 6.7. Athens. AR 'New Style' tetradrachms Obverses: Owl, head facing, standing on a fallen amphora, within an olive wreath border, A-ΘE and magistrates' names in the fields, ME in exergue. (a) *Left*: struck 134/3 BCE, 30mm, 16.79 gm, magistrates Timarchos, Nikago(ras), and Antiochos; anchor with a star to the left; K on the amphora,. Thompson no. 368e. CNG Triton Auction 114 (3 January 2011), lot 209. (b) *Right*: Struck 131/0 BCE, 31mm, 16.86 gm, magistrates Antiochos, Karaichos, and Skymnos; elephant to the right, E on the amphora. Thompson 397k; *SNG Copenhagen* 14, no. 212 (same dies). CNG Auction 84 (5 May 2010), lot 464. Courtesy of Classical Numismatic Group Inc.

be reflected in the 'New Style' Athenian tetradrachms, a few of which include an Antiochus as one of the mint magistrates. The fact that these particular issues also feature an anchor or an elephant, two favourite Seleucid emblems from the earliest days of the Seleucid monarchy, makes it an intriguing possibility that these coins were intended to advertise a royal Seleucid connection. Among the Seleucid kings, the most likely candidate would be Antiochus VII *Sidetes*, who ruled from 138 to 129 BCE and who might have been honoured with a mint magistracy. Sure enough, a decree mentioning a statue of Antiochus VII as standing in the Agora has been found in Athens [Habicht 2006, 168-69].

Probably, during his reign, his nephew, Antiochus VIII *Gryphus* (born in 141 BCE) was sent by his mother, Cleopatra Thea, to Athens to be educated [Appian, *Syriaca* 68]. Fittingly, a dichalkon struck by Cleopatra Thea and Antiochus VIII emulates the principal motif of the 'New Style' tetradrachms, an owl standing on a fallen amphora.

Antiochus VIII Epiphanes, nicknamed *Gryphus* ("hook-nose"; sole reign, 121/0-97/6 BCE) [Grainger 1997, 31-32; *SC* 2.1, 483-84] was about 20 years old when he assumed sole rule of the Seleucid kingdom. After a few years of relative tranquillity, in 114/3 his half-brother by Cleopatra Thea (in her marriage to Antiochus VII) invaded the Seleucid kingdom as Antiochus IX, nicknamed *Cyzicenus*. *Gryphus* beat a tactical retreat to Aspendus in Pamphylia.

There he recruited troops to top up his forces and prepared for a counter-offensive. In 112 BCE he defeated *Cyzicenus* outside Antioch. After a successful siege, he entered Antioch and, although *Cyzicenus* had managed to escape, *Gryphus* captured and murdered the queen of his rival, Cleopatra IV, at the behest of his wife, Cleopatra Tryphaena.

In 110/109 BCE the tables were turned in this power struggle and now it was *Cyzicenus* who had Tryphaena executed. From then on there was a stalemate between the two rivals, which resulted in the partition of the Seleucid kingdom between them, with *Cyzicenus* mostly dominant in the south of the country and *Gryphus* holding the rest. But the situation on the ground was not static, with territory changing hands all the time and this is reflected in the coinage of cities which operated mints. Thus, for example, in Antioch, at least three separate reigns for *Gryphus* and *Cyzicenus* can be distinguished from the coins.

In 102 BCE, Antiochus VIII *Gryphus* married Cleopatra Selene, a former consort of Ptolemy IX Soter II of Egypt and younger sister of his first wife, Cleopatra Tryphaena. Six years later, he was assassinated by Herakleion, one of his ministers, who tried to replace *Gryphus*. In a short space of time, the assassin was swept aside by *Cyzicenus*, who seized Antioch.

The continuous war between the two half-brothers sapped the strength and resources of the Seleucid kingdom. It marked its inexorable disintegration, which was accelerated by the assumption

Ill. 6.8. Cleopatra Thea and Antiochos VIII *Gryphus* (125-121 BCE). Æ (19 mm, 4.98 gm). Antioch mint. Dated SE 191 = 122/1 BCE. Diademed head of Antiochos VIII right / Owl standing on a fallen amphora. The Greek inscription reads ΒΑΣΙΛΙΣΣΗΣ ΚΛΕΟΠΑΤΡΑΣ ΘΕΑΣ [ΚΑΙ] ΒΑΣΙΛΕΩΣ ΑΝΤΙΟΧΟΥ, "of Queen Cleopatra Thea (goddess) [and] King Antiochus". In exergue, ΑϘΡ (date) and *aphlaston* (aplustre). *SC* no. 2263.4b.

Ill. 6.9. Antiochus VIII Epiphanes *Gryphus* (121/0-97/6 BCE). AR tetradrachms (29 mm,16.62 gm and 28 mm, 15.78 gm, respectively). Antioch mint. *Obverse*: Diademed head of Antiochus VIII. The Greek reverse inscription reads ΒΑΣΙΛΕΩΣ ΑΝΤΙΟΧΟΥ (right) ΕΠΙΦΑΝΟΥΣ (left), "of King Antiochus *Epiphanes* (the illustrious)". (a) **Above**: Struck 121-113 BCE. *Reverse*: Zeus, crescent above head, standing, holding star and sceptre; monograms IE above A to the left and A to the right; all set within an olive wreath border. *SC* no. 2298.2f (b) **Below**: Struck c. 109-96 BCE. *Reverse*: Zeus seated, holding a Nike offering a wreath in his right hand and a sceptre in his left; monograms P over E above, and another, A, below the throne, all within an laurel wreath border. *SC* no. 2309.1a. The lower coin clearly shows a considerably older Antiochus VIII.

The full titles of Antiochus VIII were Epiphanes Philomator Callinicus ("the illustrious, mother-loving, of noble victory"), as recorded in an inscription from Delos [*SC* 2, p. 487].

The internecine struggle between Antiochus VIII *Gryphus* and his half-brother Antiochus IX *Cyzicenus* prevented either Seleucid king from acting effectively against John *Hyrcanus* and countering the expansion of Hasmonaean Judaea [Josephus, *AJ* 13.270, 273-274]. Indeed, neither rival was able to respond decisively to the pleas of the inhabitants of Samaria and lift a siege mounted on the city by *Hyrcanus* and his sons Antigonus and Aristobulus [Josephus, *BJ* 1.65; *AJ* 13.276-277]. Cyzicenus petitioned Ptolemy IX Soter II *Lathyrus* for military aid against *Hyrcanus*, but the 6,000 men sent by Ptolemy proved ineffectual [Josephus, *AJ* 13.278-279].

of autonomy by cities on the coast and the divorce of entire provinces from the Seleucid state.

Principal Ancient Sources:
Appian, *Syriaca* 68-69.
Athenaeus, 153B-C; 2146D; 540A-B.
Eusebius, *Chronicon* pp.258-259.
Josephus, *Bellum Judaicum* (*BJ*) 1.65.
Josephus, *Antiquitates Judaicae* (*AJ*) 13. 270-274, 276-279, 365
Justin, *Epitome* 39.1-4.

Antiochus IX Philopator (114/3-95 BCE) [Grainger 1997, 32-33; *SC* 2.1, 521-22] received his nickname ***Cyzicenus*** (Cyzicus) from the town in Asia Minor where he was placed by his mother, Cleopatra Thea, during the second reign of his stepfather, Demetrius II. He gained a reputation as a *bon viveur*, enjoying his alcohol and luxury. *Cyzicenus* was much taken to the performing arts of play acting, mime, puppetry and conjuring. He was also fond of hunting, slipping out at night with a servant or two to hunt lions, leopards and boars.

Between 113 BCE and 95 BCE, Antioch was intermittently held by the forces of *Cyzicenus*, but his main power base lay in the south, including the cities of Damascus, Sidon and Ake-Ptolemais, which he held for a number of years, according to coin evidence. The arrival at

Ill. 6.10. Antiochus IX Philopator *Cyzicenus* (114/3-95 BCE). AR tetradrachms (29 mm, 16.40 gm and 28 mm, 16.24 gm, respectively). Antioch mint. *Obverse*: Diademed head of Antiochus IX. The Greek reverse inscription reads ΒΑΣΙΛΕΩΣ ΑΝΤΙΟΧΟΥ (left) ΦΙΛΟΠΑΤΟΡΟΣ (right), "of King Antiochus *Philopator* (father-loving)". (1) ***Above***: Struck 113-112 BCE. *Reverse*: Athena Nicephorus standing, holding a Nike in her right hand, and a shield and spear in her left; monograph at outer left; all set within an olive wreath border. The choice of Athena is surely meant to present Antiochus IX as the son and heir of Antiochus VII *Sidetes*. *SC* no. 2363b. (2) ***Below***: Struck 96/5 BCE. *Reverse*: Zeus seated, holding a Nike offering a wreath in his right hand and a sceptre in his left; monograms E over Λ above A and another below the throne, all within laurel wreath. *SC* no. 2369.3c. The lower coin bears a much older portrait of Antiochus IX, with a fuller face, including a double chin.

his court of Cleopatra IV, who had been estranged from her husband Ptolemy IX Soter II, with troops from Cyprus, boosted his position for a while. Antiochus IX married her and she may have been the mother of the future Antiochus X.

In c.107 BCE, the Hasmonaean leader, John *Hyrcanus* laid siege to Samaria, the inhabitants of which twice appealed to *Cyzicenus* for aid. *Cyzicenus* obtained a detachment of 6,000 men to help relieve Samaria. Unable to relieve Samaria, these troops instead ravaged Judaean territory and many of them fell in ambushes laid by *Hyrcanus*. Impatient with the lack of progress in his campaign, *Cyzicenus* went off to Tripolis, leaving two of his officers in charge, and after a year's siege, Samaria fell to *Hyrcanus* [Josephus, *Antiquitates Judaicae* 13.275-280].

Following the demise of his rival, Antiochus *Gryphus*, *Cyzicenus* established himself in Antioch for a third time in 96 BCE and married his widow, Cleopatra Selene. Then, *Gryphus'* son, Seleucus VI, arrived on the scene to claim the throne; he managed to capture Antioch and do away with his uncle before the year 95 BCE was out.

According to the documentary and numismatic evidence, John *Hyrcanus* I further expanded Judaean territory annexing areas of Transjordan to the east, as well as the district and city of Samaria and beyond to Scythopolis (Beth-shean) to the north and Idumaea (Edom) to the south. He forced the Idumaeans to convert to Judaism [Josephus, *BJ* 1.63-66; *AJ* 255-258]. As with regard to Samaria, these campaigns drew only a few ineffective incursions from Antiochus *Cyzicenus* [*AJ* 13.275-283]. Hyrcanus seems to have been emboldened by a vision that he had while officiating as High Priest in the Temple of his victorious army, which is recorded in Josephus and rabbinical sources [Josephus, *AJ* 13.282-283; Tosefta, *Sotah* 13.5; Jerusalem Talmud, *Sotah* 24b; Babylonian Talmud, *Sotah* 33a].

Hyrcanus ruled with the support of the Sadducees, one of the three main factions or religious parties that emerged during the rule of Jonathan the Maccabee, according to Josephus [*AJ* 13.171-173]. The other 'sects' are the Pharisees and Essenes. While Josephus emphasises the difference between the Pharisees and the Sadducees with regard to their respective attitudes towards preordained fate and free will, in rabbinical tradition, they are differentiated by the insistence of the Pharisees in the equal validity of the Oral Law and that specifically written in the Bible, whereas the Sadducees only accepted the Written Law and they did not believe in resurrection of the dead, unlike the Pharisees. The Pharisees developed out of the *Hasidim*, the pietist group which had supported the Maccabaean insurgency, while the Sadducees were strongly associated with the priestly aristocracy and grandees. Ruling out notions of providence and fatalism, they believed that one's actions lie entirely within our power, a prescription that chimed well with the pragmatic Hasmonaeans. On the other hand, the

Essenes were an ascetic sect which generally dwelt apart from the Jewish mainstream. They had stringent rules for initiates and members and their particular purification ritual and adoption of a solar calendar which was out of kilter with that observed by other Jews caused them to be excluded from the Temple in Jerusalem [Josephus, *BJ* 2.119-166 *AJ* 13.297-298; 18.12-20].

Hyrcanus openly declared himself hostile to the Pharisees over their uncompromising demand that he should give up the high priesthood and be content with being political ruler of Judaea [Josephus, *AJ* 13.288-298].

Apparently, Hyrcanus desired that his wife (whose name is unknown to us) succeed him as head of the government, with his eldest of five sons, Judah Aristobulus, initially only assuming the high priesthood [Josephus, *BJ* 1.70-71; *AJ* 13.299-302]. According to Josephus, Judah Aristobulus I (ruled 104-103 BCE) was the first Hasmonaean ruler to wear the royal diadem and proclaim himself king, but Strabo [16.2.40] says that Alexander Jannaeus, his younger brother and successor, was the first to do so. From the coin evidence, it appears that Strabo is correct on this point (see below). We are also told that Aristobulus I bore the epithet, *Philhellene* (= friend of the Greeks), which reflected his leanings.

Upon *Hyrcanus'* death, Judah Aristobulus I jailed his mother and three brothers, including Alexander Jannaeus, and allowed her to starve in prison. According to the same source, out of envy he turned on his favourite brother, Antigonus, and had him murdered. This disparaging picture of Aristobulus could be slander generated by his detractors, being at complete variance with that painted by another source, the 1st century BCE Alexandrian historian and rhetorician, Timagenes, quoted third-hand by Josephus via Strabo, who described Aristobulus as "a kindly person" and a benefactor of the Jews, "for he acquired additional territory for them and brought over to them a portion of the Ituraean nation, whom he joined to them by the bond of circumcision" [Josephus, *AJ* 13.319]. This is a curious statement because the Ituraeans inhabited inland territory to the north of Galilee, roughly corresponding to the eastern half of modern Lebanon, and rather distant from Judaea. No mention is made in the ancient sources about the incorporation of Galilee into the Hasmonaean kingdom, but the fact that no attempt to oblige the Galileans to adopt Judaism and be circumcised is referred to may be significant. The archaeological evidence is consistent with the settlement of Jewish immigrants in Galilee. The region seems to have been largely vacated by its previous gentile inhabitants, either peacefully or by force – or by a combination of these two means – followed by the absorption of Galilee into the Hasmonaean realm during the reign of Judah Aristobulus I or that of his brother or successor, Alexander Jannaeus.

The latter had close-hand familiarity with Galilee if, as we are told, he had spent his early years there [Josephus, *AJ* 13.322].

Aristobulus I died one year later after a painful illness in 103 BCE. His surviving brothers were freed from prison by his widow, Salome-Salina Alexandra, who then married Jannaeus, his successor [Josephus, *BJ* 1.70-85; *AJ* 13.301-323].

Principal Ancient Sources:
Appian, *Syriaca* 68-69.
Diodorus Siculus, 34/35.34.
Eusebius, *Chronicon* pp.257-259.
Josephus, *Bellum Judaicum* (*BJ*) 1.70-85.
Josephus, *Antiquitates Judaicae* (*AJ*) 13.275-281, 301-323, 365-366.
Justin, *Epitome* 39.2-4.
Strabo, *Geographia* 16.2.40.

CHAPTER 7.

FROM SELEUCUS VI TO ANTIOCHUS XII – DISINTEGRATION OF THE SELEUCID KINGDOM AND ESTABLISHMENT OF THE HASMONAEAN MONARCHY

Seleucus VI Epiphanes Nicator (96/5-94/3 BCE) [Grainger 1997, 65; *SC* 2.1, 551], the eldest son of Antiochus VIII by Cleopatra Selene, declared himself Seleucid king, first in western Cilicia, while he prepared for his campaign to take Antioch and overthrow his uncle, Antiochus IX *Cyzicenus*.

This he achieved in 96/95 BCE, but less than a year later he was driven out of Antioch by Antiochus X, the son of Antiochus IX. Seleucus was chased westwards to Mopsus (Mopsuestia) in Cilicia but his tyrannical conduct and his heavy financial exactions from the populace precipitated an uprising in that city. In the tumult, Seleucus along with members of his inner circle ('Friends') were caught in his residence or city's gymnasium and burned to death.

Seleucus VI combined the epithets of his father Antiochus VIII (Epiphanes) and his grandfather Demetrius II (Nicator).

Principal Ancient Sources:
Appian, *Syriaca* 69.
Eusebius, *Chronicon* pp.259-261.
Josephus, *Antiquitates Judaicae* (*AJ*) 13.366-368, 370.

Ill. 7.1. Seleucus VI Epiphanes Nicator (c.96/5-94/3 BCE). AR tetradrachms (27 mm, 15.65 gm and 28 mm, 15.99 gm, respectively). Diademed head of Seleucus VI / (a) ***Above***: Athena standing, holding a Nike in her right hand and a shield and spear on her left, with a monogram and 'ZH' to the left and a flower to the outer left. Seleucia-on-the-Calycadnus (Cilicia) mint. *SC* no. 2405.1; (b) ***Below***: Zeus seated, holding a Nike offering a wreath in his right hand and a sceptre in his left; letters and monogram at the outer left: and Π (bottom) under the throne; all set within an olive wreath border. Antioch mint. *SC* no. 2415c. The Greek inscription on both coins reads ΒΑΣΙΛΕΩΣ ΣΕΛΕΥΚΟΥ (right side) ΕΠΙΦΑΝΟΥΣ ΝΙΚΑΤΟΡΟΣ (left side), "of King Seleucus *Epiphanes Nicator* (illustrious and victorious)". The portrait on the upper coin is more naturalistic than on the one shown below.

Antiochus X Eusebes Philopator (c.94-c. 88 BCE) [Grainger 1997, 33-34; *SC* 2.1, 565-55], the son of Antiochus IX Cyzicenus and possibly of Cleopatra IV, declared himself king at the Phoenician town of Aradus. He took as his wife Cleopatra Selene, the widow of his father and also of his uncle, Antiochus VIII Gryphus. No sooner had he established himself in power than he was targeted by Seleucus VI's younger brothers, Antiochus XI Philadelphus and Philip I Philadelphus. The ancient sources tend to be rather murky about Antiochus X's reign; there are contradictions and their information cannot be taken at face value.

What can be stated with reasonable confidence is that Antiochus XI Philadelphus and Philip I Philadelphus appeared on the scene, proclaiming their joint rule, and they sacked Mopsus (also known as Mopsuestia) to avenge the death of their older brother Seleucus VI at the hands of the angry mob. Next, Antiochus XI moved on to Syria to have a showdown with Antiochus X. The latter got the better of his cousin in battle and Antiochus XI is said to have drowned in the River Orontes while attempting to escape. It seems that Antiochus XI occupied and reigned very briefly at Antioch in 94/3 BCE, before being driven out by Antiochus X. In c. 88 BCE, Antiochus X died in battle while fighting the Parthians.

The combined reigns of John *Hyrcanus* I, Judah Aristobulus I and Alexander Jannaeus overlapped the reigns of no less than fifteen squabbling Seleucid kings, all descendants of Demetrius I Soter. This chronic instability took a heavy toll on the Seleucid kingdom, which is reflected in its coinage. A noticeable reduction occurs in the weight of the silver coins while

Ill. 7.2. Antiochos X Eusebes Philopator (c.94-c.88 BCE). AR tetradrachm (27 mm, 15.74 gm). Antioch mint, c. 94 BCE. Diademed head of Antiochos X / Zeus seated, holding a Nike offering a wreath in his right hand and a sceptre in his left; to the outer left and below the throne are control monograms; set within an olive wreath border. The Greek inscription reads ΒΑΣΙΛΕΩΣ ΑΝΤΙΟΧΟΥ (right side) ΕΥΣΕΒΟΥΣ [Φ]ΙΛΟΠΑΤΟΡΟΣ (left side), "of King Antiochus *Eusebes Philopator* (the pious and father-loving)". *SC* no. 2429.1a.

the quality of the silver itself is distinctly inferior (i.e. adulterated with base metals) and a sharp decline is evident in their artistic merit. Local Semitic deities now feature prominently on Seleucid issues and serve as an illustration of the assimilation of the Seleucid monarchy into the local Levantine environment.

Alexander Jannaeus, a younger son of John *Hyrcanus*, reigned from 103 to 76 BCE. Jannaeus, the Greek transliteration of the Hebrew Yannai, is a diminutive form for Jonathan, as his coins make clear. A power vacuum in the Mediterranean during the first quarter of the 1st century BCE provided an environment that enabled expansion of the Hasmonaean kingdom with little opposition. The Seleucids were wracked by internecine strife, the Ptolemies were beset by similar discord between sons of Ptolemy VIII *Physcon*, Ptolemy IX *Lathyrus* (who held Egypt intermittently between 116 and 81 BCE) and his brother, Ptolemy X Alexander. Rome entered a period of instability, with the onset of civil war in 88 BCE.

Jannaeus managed to extended the territory of Judaea along the coast from the coast of Philistia to the Carmel and in Transjordan from north of Panias (Banias) to Machaerus on the eastern shore of the Dead Sea. His conquest of Gaza, Anthedon and Raphia on the coast of Philistia gave the Hasmonaean kingdom control of the main Nabataean trade-route outlet to the Mediterranean which ignited a war with the Nabataean kingdom. He launched a campaign

Ill. 7.3. Antiochos X Eusebes Philopator. Æ 4 chalkoi (20 mm, 8.69 gm). Antioch mint. c. 94 BCE. Diademed head of Antiochus X, with a beard / Caps (*piloi*) of the Dioscuri surmounted by stars; grape bunch to the inner left, monogram to the outer right. The Greek inscription reads ΒΑΣΙΛΕΩ[Σ] ΑΝΤΙΟΧΟ[Υ] (right side) ΕΥΣΕΒΟΥ[Σ] [ΦΙ]ΛΟΠΑΤΟΡ[ΟΣ] (left side). *SC* no. 2432.2b.

Ill. 7.4. Demetrius III Theos Philopator Soter *Eucaerus* (97/6-88/7 BCE). AR Tetradrachm (27 mm, 15.43 gm). Antioch mint, c. 96-87 BC. Diademed head right / Zeus enthroned left, holding a Nike offering a wreath in his right hand and a sceptre in his left; set within an olive wreath border; to the outer left and below the throne are control monograms. The Greek inscription reads ΒΑΣΙΛΕΩΣ ΔΗΜΗΤΡΙΟΥ ΘΕΟΥ (right side) ΦΙΛΟΠΑΤΟΡΟΣ ΣΩΤΗΡΟΣ (left side), "of King Demetrius *Theos Philopator Soter* (father-loving – referring to Antiochus VIII *Gryphus* – god and saviour)". *SC* no. 2445. Roma Numismatics E-Sale 16 (28 February 2015), lot 241. Courtesy of Roma Numismatics.

The epithet Soter ("saviour") is likely to refer to Demetrius' protection of the population of Damascus from the threats of Ituraeans, Nabataeans and Judaeans who were pressing on Damascus from all sides.

against the city of Ake-Ptolemais, which called on Ptolemy *Lathyrus* for help. Jannaeus was saved from almost certain defeat by the timely intervention from *Lathyrus*' mother, Cleopatra III, who was at odds with her son. Jannaeus continued the practice of his father of relying on foreign mercenaries, in his case recruited from Pisidia and Cilicia in southern Asia Minor. Judging from the rather undistinguished performance of Jannaeus' army, as one might expect, the mercenaries lacked the motivation of the locally recruited men who had fought with the Maccabees for their freedom [Josephus, *BJ* 1.86-90; *AJ* 13.324-364].

Principal Ancient Sources:
Appian, *Syriaca* 69.
Eusebius, *Chronicon* pp. 260-261.
Josephus, *Bellum Judaicum* (*BJ*) 1.86-90.
Josephus, *Antiquitates Judaicae* (*AJ*) 13.324-364, 367, 369-371.

Demetrius III Philopator Soter *Eucaerus* (97/6- 88/7 BCE) [Grainger 1997, 44; *SC* 2.1, 581-82], a younger son of Antiochus VIII Gryphus was helped to the throne at Damascus by Ptolemy IX Soter (*Lathyrus*), from his retreat in Cnidus.

Coins struck in Damascus by Demetrius show that this occurred in 97/6 BCE. By taking this action from his exile in Cyprus, the Ptolemaic king circumvented Damascus being occupied by Antiochus IX *Cyzicenus* or some local leader. Demetrius III's nickname *Eucaerus* means "well-timed", possibly a misunderstanding of the derogative Greek epithet *Akairos*, "the untimely one". Both forms are applied to him in Josephus.

When Antiochus X regained Antioch after the death of their brother Antiochus XI, Demetrius III *Eucaerus* and Philip I Philadelphus moved against him and when he died while fighting the Parthians, Syria was carved up between Demetrius and Philip.

During the reign of Alexander Jannaeus (103-76 BCE), his exasperated Jewish subjects drew Demetrius III into a dispute against their unpopular ruler [Josephus, *BJ* 1.92-95; *AJ* 13.370-371, 376-379]. Demetrius defeated Jannaeus in battle near Shechem, but then withdrew when the majority of Jews, who had earlier opposed Jannaeus, rallied to his side. We next find Demetrius III besieging Beroea (Aleppo) in 88/7 BCE pursuit against his brother Philip I. He brought with him Antiochene troops on this campaign, indicating that Demetrius was then occupying the Seleucid capital. The local ruler of Beroea, Straton, was an ally of Philip and called in support from Azizus, an Arab chieftain, and Mithradates Sinakes, the Parthian governor of Mesopotamia. They succeeded in overwhelming Demetrius' camp, captured him and dispatched Demetrius to Mithradates II of Parthia, who held him under comfortable 'house arrest' in his court, until his natural death.

Ill. 7.5. Demetrius III Theos Philopator Soter *Eucaerus* . AR tetradrachm (28 mm, 15.19 gm). Damascus mint. Diademed head of Demetrius III / Cult statue of Atargatis facing frontally; olive wreath border at the very edge of the field. The Greek inscription reads ΒΑΣΙΛΕΩΣ ΔΗΜΗΤΡΙΟΥ ΘΕΟΥ (right side) ΦΙΛΟΠΑΤΟΡΟΣ ΣΩΤΗΡΟΣ (left side), "of King Demetrius *Theos Philopator Soter* (father-loving god and saviour)". In left field, N to the right and two monograms to the left of the main inscription. In exergue, ΔΚΣ = 224 SE (89/88 BCE) and monogram |Δ|. *SC* no. 2451.11.

Atargatis was the Syrian goddess of fertility and also the protector of cities and their populations. Here, she is represented with the body of a fish and veiled, with an egg on her chest and flanked by barley stalks, symbolising fertility. An Atargateion (temple to Atargatis) existed at Carnion (Qarnaim) in Gilead, according to 2 Macc. 12.26 (cf. 1 Macc. 5.43).

Late in his reign Jannaeus expanded the Hasmonaean kingdom east of the Jordan, occupying the cities of Gerasa, Gamala and Pella. The last of these was destroyed because its inhabitants refused to adopt Jewish customs [Josephus, *AJ* 13.393-397].

Although Alexander Jannaeus presented himself as the champion of the Jewish cause, he was unpopular among the majority of his own subjects who had support from the Pharisaic faction. While officiating at the Altar in the Temple during a festival of Tabernacles, he was pelted with citrons by hostile worshippers. In revenge for this and other acts of insubordination, Jannaeus wreaked revenge with acts of extreme cruelty against his own Jewish subjects. In c. 93 BCE, he and his Sadducean supporters became embroiled in a six year civil war with the alienated Jewish majority, backed by the Pharisees, during which Demetrius III *Eucaerus* was drawn in to the internal conflict. At the end of the civil war, Jannaeus wreaked punitive revenge, which included the crucifixion of 800 rebels in Jerusalem. This episode is touched on in the Commentary of Nahum contained within the Dead Sea Scrolls [4Q169]. Demetrius is named there as is the terrible retribution wrought by "the furious young lion" (Alexander Jannaeus, who hanged his protagonists alive "on the tree", i.e. crucified them).

Jannaeus fell ill from heavy drinking and died during the siege of the fortress Ragaba, while on campaign against the Nabataeans [Josephus, *BJ* 1.88-106; *AJ* 13.372-406]. He was just 49 years old.

Principal Ancient Sources:
Josephus, *Bellum Judaicum* (*BJ*) 1.88-106.
Josephus, *Antiquitates Judaicae* (*AJ*) 13.370-406.

Philip I Epiphanes Philadelphus (95/4-c.76/5 BCE) [Grainger 1997, 52; *SC* 2.1, 595-96] was a younger son of Antiochus VIII Gryphus and Cleopatra Tryphaena, and brother of four other Seleucid monarchs, Seleucus VI, Antiochus XI, Demetrius III and Antiochus XII. The numismatic evidence indicates that he remained in Cilicia when his older brother Antiochus XI proceeded east to Antioch to challenge Antiochus X Eusebes. Following the early death of his brother, Philip appears to have extended his rule over part of Syria, while another sibling, Demetrius III, held Damascus and the south.

After Philip's successful rebuff of Demetrius at Beroea, he established himself at Antioch. Meanwhile, the vacuum at Damascus was quickly filled by another brother, Antiochus XII, before Philip could make a move on that city. Another opportunity for Philip came when Antiochus was away from Damascus, campaigning against the Nabataeans. Philip marched on Damascus with an army and the city was yielded to him by Milesius, the guardian of its citadel. This deed went 'unappreciated' by Philip, so Milesius had a change of heart and shut him out of the city when Philip left it to visit the local hippodrome.

Philip's reign at Antioch seems to have come to an end by 76/5 BCE. According to Cicero [*In Verrem* 4.61], Cleopatra Selene sent her two sons to Rome to seek recognition from the Senate of their legitimacy as kings of Syria and Egypt, respectively. In the absence of objections to the Syrian claim from any quarter, it is probable that the throne of Syria was vacant at that time; Tigranes II of Armenia had not yet reached this region.

Principal Ancient Sources:
Appian, *Syriaca* 48.
Cicero, *In Verrem* 4.61.
Eusebius, *Chronicon* pp.261.
Josephus, *Antiquitates Judaicae* (*AJ*) 13.369-371, 384-389.

Antiochus XII Dionysos Epiphanes Philopator Callinicus (c. 87/6-83/2 BCE) [Grainger 1997, 34; *SC* 2.1, 607] was the last of the Seleucid rulers to challenge the Hasmonaean state. He was the youngest son of Antiochus VIII *Gryphus* and Cleopatra Tryphaena, who seized control of Damascus in 87/6 BCE, after his brother Demetrius III was taken into captivity in Parthia. Antiochus was the first king of the Seleucid dynasty who made no attempt to gain control of its hereditary capital, Antioch, and engage in the affairs of northern Syria. Instead, Antiochus XII focused his attention on his neighbours to the south, namely Hasmonaean Judaea and the Nabataean kingdom.

Ill. 7.6. Philip I Epiphanes Philadelphus (c.95/4-c.76/5 BCE). AR tetradrachm (28 mm, 16.09 gm), struck in 88/7-76/5 BCE. Antioch mint. Diademed head of Philip I / Zeus Nikephoros seated, holding a Nike offering a wreath in his right hand and a sceptre in his left; all set within an olive wreath border; to outer left, Φ above A; monogram(s) below the throne. The Greek inscription reads ΒΑΣΙΛΕΩΣ ΦΙΛΙΠΠΟΥ (right side), ΕΠΙΦΑΝΟΥΣ ΦΙΛΑΔΕΛΦΟΥ (left side), "of King Philip *Ephiphanes Philadelphus* (illustrious, brother-loving" – the brother in question being Antiochus XI Epiphanes Philadelphus, his partner as joint ruler at the outset in 94/93 BCE). *SC* no. 2463.3a.

Ill. 7.7. Antiochus XII Dionysus Epiphanes Philopator Callinicus (c. 87/6-83/2 BCE). Damascus mint.

(a) **Above:** Æ tetrachalkon (21 mm, 8.17 g). Diademed and draped bust of Antiochus XII / Zeus Aëtophoros standing left. monogram in exergue. The Greek inscription reads ΒΑΣΙΛΕΩΣ ΑΝΤΙΟΧΟΥ ΔΙΗ(!)ΟΝΥΣΟΥ (right side) ΕΠΙΦΑΝΟΥΣ ΦΙΛΟΠΑΤΟΡΟΣ ΚΑΛΛΙΝΙΚΟΥ (left side), "of King Antiochus *Dionysus Epiphanes Philopator Callinicus* (Dionysus manifest, father-loving – referring to Antiochus VIII *Gryphus* – and nobly victorious"). *SC* no. 2481.
(b) **Below:** Æ dichalkon (17 mm, 4.28 gm). Diademed head of Antiochus, XII / Nike advancing right, holding wreath and palm; monogram to outer left. The Greek inscription reads ΒΑΣΙΛΕΩ[Σ] ΑΝΤΙΟΧΟΥ ΕΠΙΦΑΝΟΥ[Σ] (right side) ΦΙΛΟΠΑΤΟΡΟ[Σ] ΚΑΛΛΙΝΙΚ[ΟΥ] (left side), "of King Antiochus Epiphanes Philopator Callinicus". *SC* no. 2479.

On both coins, Antiochus XII is shown with a short curly beard, like his elder brother Demetrius III, indicative of a vow taken by the king, which when fulfilled would be signified by its removal. These issues are believed to date from the second half of his reign; his earlier coins depict him clean-shaven.

During his first campaign against Nabataea, Antiochus XII's brother Philip briefly occupied Damascus but was then ejected. This experience did not deter Antiochus resuming his campaign in the south and his army descended on Judaea on its way to attack the Nabataean kingdom. Seeing this encroachment as a direct threat to his kingdom, Alexander Jannaeus threw up extensive defence-works to thwart the Seleucid forces. Antiochus XII swept aside this barrier and continued on to Arabia through Judaean territory [Josephus, *BJ* 1.99-100; *AJ* 13.389-391]. The Nabataeans, led by Aretas III, confronted the Seleucid army. In the ensuing battle, the army of Antiochus XII was initially successful, but then the young king was killed. Thereupon his soldiers fled the field. Most of them died of hunger in the desert. Now left vulnerable, Damascus fell into the hands of the Nabataean king, Aretas III, in 85 BCE thereby ending, once and for all, the chances of the Seleucids enjoying a revival and ever threatening Judaea again.

Principal Ancient Sources:
Josephus, *Bellum Judaicum* (*BJ*) 1.99-103.
Josephus, *Antiquitates Judaicae* (*AJ*) 13.387-392.

Alexander Jannaeus was followed by his wife Salome-Salina Alexandra, who reigned from 76 to 67 BCE. Salome is a shortened form of Shelamzion, and she is referred to under that name in Dead Sea Scroll fragments 4Q331-2. She served as the only reigning Jewish queen, rather following Ptolemaic and Seleucid precedents, as exemplified by Cleopatra Thea, who also married successive monarchs of the same dynasty. In Jewish tradition, her reign is viewed as the golden age of Hasmonaean Judaea [Babylonian Talmud, *Ta'anit* 23a]. She is reputed to have been the sister of the Pharisaic sage, Shimon ben Shetaḥ [Babylonian Talmud, *Berakhot* 48a]. The party of the Pharisees, which had suffered under Alexander Jannaeus, became the dominant influence at her Court. The Sanhedrin, now under the presidency of Shimon ben Shetaḥ, was reorganised and assumed the status of the Supreme Court of the Kingdom. Alexandra's son, Hyrcanus II (whose Hebrew name is not recorded), held the office of High Priest and was named as her successor.

Salome-Salina Alexandra attended to the defence of her realm, maintaining and equipping a network of fortresses. Although Judaea was mostly at peace during her reign, she sent her son Aristobulus with an army to besiege Damascus, to counter an attack on that city by the Ituraean dynast, Ptolemy Mennaeus. However, the expedition did not achieve any significant result. She succeeded in buying off the attentions of Tigranes II of Armenia on Judaea during his advance south to Ake-Ptolemais in 70/69 BCE. Towards the end of Alexander Salome's reign, her younger son, Aristobulus, attempted to seize control of the kingdom, which he succeeded to do after her death [Josephus, *BJ* 1.107-119; *AJ* 13.407-432].

Whereas John *Hyrcanus* I and Judah Aristobulus I refer to themselves on their coins only as High Priests, Alexander Jannaeus styles himself 'King' on his later coins. The wreath border enclosing the ruler's name and title (following a convention widely applied to Seleucid and other Hellenistic coins from about the mid-2nd century BCE – but without their portraits), is joined during Jannaeus' reign by a royal diadem [*TJC*, 37-38]. This and the starburst inscribed in the ring-like diadem are emphatic statements of Hellenistic-style royal authority. Here, we have graphic evidence that it was Alexander Jannaeus and not Judah Aristobulus I who was the first Hamonaean ruler to declare himself king [Strabo 16. 2, 40, *contra* Josephus, *BJ* 1.70; *AJ* 13.301].

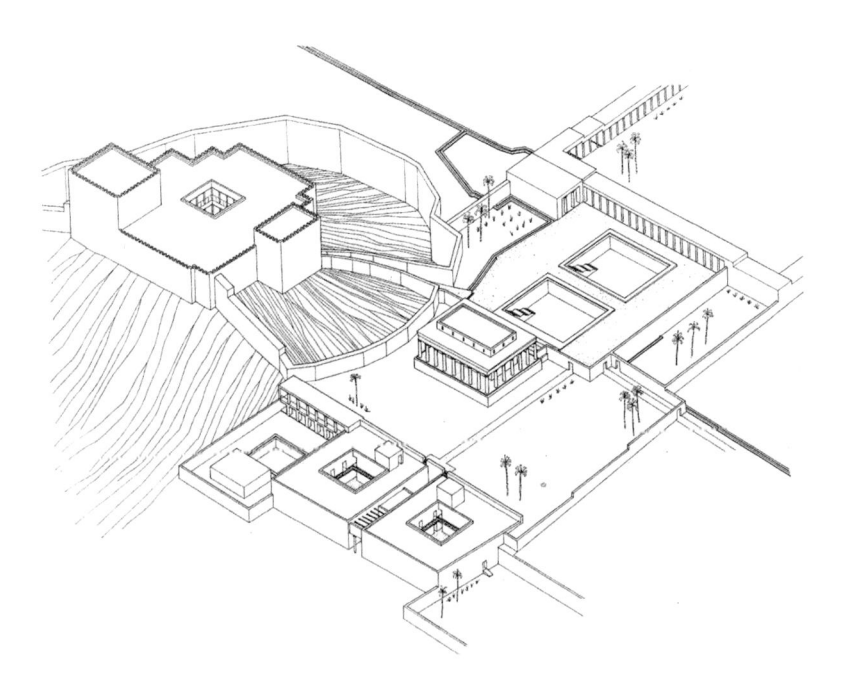

Ill. 7.8. The Hasmonaean palace complex at Tulul Abu al-'Alayiq, outside Jericho, during the reign of Salome-Salina Alexandra (76-67 BCE), as determined in archaeological excavations (Netzer 2001, 1-174; 301-311 and Ill. 457); courtesy of the late Professor Ehud Netzer. The palace buildings were designed to east-Greek norms of the period, inwardly facing on internal courtyards. The porticoes and colonnaded facades are typically Hellenistic features, while the twin pools shown on the right may reflect local tastes and priorities. Herod the Great had the last Hasmonaean high priest, Aristobulus III, drowned in one of the pools at this palace in 35 BCE [Josephus, *BJ* 1.437; *AJ* 15.56].

THE FIRST HASMONAEAN *CHALKOI* (*PRUTOT*)

A
יהוחנן
הכהן הגד(-)
(-)ל וחבר הי
הודים

Ill. 7.9. Yehoḥanan (John) *Hyrcanus* I (135-104 BCE). (a) Æ prutah/ chalkon (14 mm, 2.04 gm). Jerusalem mint. Hebrew inscription headed by 'A' within an olive wreath, which reads YHWḤNN HKHN HGDL WḤBR HY/HWDYM, "Yehochanan (John), the High Priest, and ḥever (council) of the Jews" / Double cornucopias with ribbons; pomegranate between the horns. *TJC* no. A3.

יהוד(-)
ה כהן גד
ול וחבר
היהוד(-)
ים

יהוד(-)
ה כהן גד
(-)ול וחבר ה
יהוד(-)
ים

Ill. 7.10. Yehudah (Judah) Aristobulus I (104-103 BCE). Æ prutat/ chalkoi (13 mm, 1.93 gm and 14 mm, 1.99 gm, respectively). Jerusalem mint. Hebrew inscription within an olive wreath, which reads YHWDH KHN GDL WḤBR HYHWDYM "Yehudah (Judah), High Priest, and ḥever of the Jews" / Double cornucopias with ribbons; pomegranate between the horns. (a) obverse, *TJC* no. U4; reverse, A; (b) *TJC* no. U6; reverse B.

(-) יהו
נתן הכ (-)
הן הגדל
וחב[ר] ה(-)
יה[ודים]

Ill. 7.11. Alexander (Yehonatan = Jonathan, Jannaeus) (103-76 BCE). (a) **Left (1)**: Æ prutah/ chalkon (12 mm, 1.6 gm). Jerusalem mint. Olive wreath enclosing inscription, which reads YHWNTN HKHN HGDL WḤBR HYHWDYM, "Yehonatan (Jonathan), the High Priest, and ḥever of the Jews". The reverse is the same as for the above coins. *TJC* no. P, var. (b) **Centre (2)**: Æ prutah/chalkon (14mm, 3.3 gm). Jerusalem mint. Starburst within a circular diadem, with the Hebrew inscription HMLK YHWNTN, "King Yehonatan" between the rays / Greek inscription ΒΑΣΙΛΕΩΣ ΑΛΕΞΑΝΔΡΟΥ, "of King Alexander", around an inverted anchor (Seleucid emblem). *TJC* no. K3. Note the ties and tassels of the diadem in the example **2a**. (c) **Right (3)**: Æ prutah/ chalkon (13 mm, 2.0 gm). Rose surrounded by the same Hebrew inscription (HMLK YHWNTN, "King Yehonatan"). The obverse features an anchor in a circular frame and Greek inscription ΒΑΣΙΛΕΩΣ ΑΛΕΞΑΝΔΡΟΥ. *TJC* no. N1.

Sources for the designs of the first Hasmonaean coins

As with the denominations and the weight standards of Hasmonaean coins, their designs derive from neighbouring (mostly Seleucid) issues, as shown in Table 7.1 below:

Hasmonaean coin	Probable Seleucid / autonomous city prototype
Ill. 7.12a. John *Hyrcanus* I (135-104 BCE). Æ 13 mm, 1.6 gm (prutah/ chalkon). Jerusalem mint. Reverse: Pomegranate on a stalk between facing cornucopias, to which fillets are tied. *TJC* no. A3.	Ill. 7.12b. Alexander II Zabinas (128-122 BCE). Æ 19 mm, 6.10 gm (trichalkon). Alexander II Antioch mint. Reverse: Filleted entwined double cornucopias; ΒΑΣΙΛΕΩΣ / ΑΛΕΞΑΝΔΡΟΥ, "of King Alexander". *SC* no. 2235,1a.
Ill. 7.12c. John *Hyrcanus* I (135-104 BCE). Same coin as above. Obverse: Palaeo-Hebrew inscription on four lines: YHWḤNN /HKHN HGD/L WḤBR HY/HWDYM, "Yehoḥanan (John), the High Priest, and ḥever (council) of the Jews", with the letter 'A' above, within a wreath. The 'A' may refer to Alexander II Zabinas. *TJC* no. A3.	Ill. 7.12d. Antiochos VI Dionysus (144-142 BCE). Æ 17mm, 3.69 gm (dichalkon). Uncertain mint. Reverse: ΒΑΣΙΛΕΩ[Σ] ΑΝΤΙΟΧΟΥ ΕΠΙΦΑΝ[ΟΥΣ] ΔΙΟΝΥΣΟΥ, "of King Antiochus *Epiphanes Dionysos*" in four lines within ivy wreath. *SC* no. 2019. CNG e-Auction 316 (4 December 2013), lot 185. Courtesy of Classical Numismatic Group Inc.

Hasmonaean coin	Probable Seleucid / autonomous city prototype
Ill. 7.12e. John *Hyrcanus* I. Æ 12 mm, 1.1 gm (half-prutah/ hemichalkon). Jerusalem mint: Reverse: Palm branch with a strip of cloth (fillet band) tied to its tip and a palaeo-Hebrew inscription on four lines to the left and right: YHWḤN[N] /HKHN HG/DL HḤBR /HYHDY[M], "Yehoḥanan the High Priest, and ḥever of the Jews". *TJC* no. C7.	Ill. 7.12f. Tyre (autonomous issue). AR 12 mm, 1.75 gm (hemidrachm). Reverse: Palm branch with a fillet band tied to its tip; TYRIΩN (of Tyre) across field; below, LI = CY 10 = 117/6 BCE, *beth* and monogram. Unpublished. NAC Auction 64 (17 May 2012), lot 1517. Courtesy of Numismatica Ars Classica NAC AG.

Table 7.1. Hasmonaean coin motifs and their likely models

Features of Hasmonaean Coinage

The Hasmonaean kings only minted bronze coins of the small chalkon (prutah) denomination for everyday purchases, relying on the larger bronze and higher value silver coinage of the coastal cities for larger transactions. At that time, most of the southern Levant's coinage was produced at Tyre, which enjoyed a high degree of autonomy from 126 BCE to 65 CE [see *RPC* I, 655-56]. Its silver shekels and half-shekels were relatively pure (~95% silver). Sidon also minted shekels until 30/29 BCE, and half-shekels, occasionally, until 43/44 CE, but not on a similar scale [*RPC* I, 651]. The high quality of Tyrian silver may account for the Temple treasury requiring the temple tax levied on all male Jews over the age of twenty, being stipulated in Tyrian half-shekels, despite the pagan images of the city's chief deity, Melqart-Hercules, on its obverse and an eagle, symbol of Zeus, on its reverse (see Ill. 8.1). This silver currency may have also been chosen by the Temple authorities because it was the most prevalent form of silver coinage available when the Temple Tax was instituted, which would have been sometime during the Hasmonaean period [Baumgarten 1996].

Ill. 7.13. Dichalkon (2-prutot) of John *Hyrcanus* I (Æ 17 mm, 3.4 gm). Parallel conjoined cornucopias tied with ribbons; surrounding inscription in palaeo-Hebrew: YHḤNN HKHN HGDL R'Š HḤBR HYHWDYM, "Yehoḥanan (John) the High Priest and ḥ*ever* (council) of the Jews" / Crested Boeotian helmet with cheek guards. *TJC* no. H1. Heritage Auction of 9 March 2012, lot 20082. Courtesy of Heritage Auctions Inc.

Ill. 7.14. Hemichalkon (½-prutah) of John *Hyrcanus* (Æ 12 mm, 1.0 gm). Jerusalem mint. Palm branch with inscription in palaeo-Hebrew on four lines to the left and right: [YHḤNN H]KHN H[GDL] /R'Š HḤ[BR] HYHD[M], "Yehoḥanan, the High Priest, and ḥ*ever* of the Jews" / Rose between two buds. *TJC* no. J4.

Representative examples of the largest and smallest denominations struck in the name of John *Hyrcanus* (the dichalkon and hemichalkon) are illustrated here; the size, weight and denominational relationships for the series of three coins denominations issued in his name – the dichakon, chalkon and hemichalkon – are shown in Table 7.2.

The possible sources of the rose on this Hasmonaean coin are Rhodian coins. The small Rhodian diobol shown in Ill. 7.15 (a), below, bears a strikingly similar representation. Another possible iconographic source would be the handle stamps on the many Rhodian amphorae that found their way to Jerusalem, such as the one shown in Ill. 7.15 (b).

A comparison of the weights and diameters of coins in Tables 5.1 and 7.2 highlights the close denominational relationship between the coins of John *Hyrcanus* (and those of his successors), on the one hand, and contemporaneous Seleucid bronze coinage, on the other. Interestingly, the Judaean denomination that has been identified as the prutah and mentioned in rabbinical literature, equates to the Seleucid chalkon. This should, perhaps, be expected because Hasmonaean coinage evolved out of that of the Seleucids. There is even a linking coin issue, namely the prutot/chalkoi issued by John *Hyrcanus* I for Antiochus VII Sidetes (*SC* nos. 2123.1-2, illustrated in Ill. 6.3). Besides, coin hoards have amply demonstrated that there was a large overlap of geographical distribution of these coins, which are often found together. This suggests that there was a requirement for them to be readily interchangeable.

The inscription on all the John *Hyrcanus* I coins mentions the minting authority as: "Yehoḥanan the high priest and [head of] the ḥ*ever* of the Jews" (with or without the words in square brackets). This is close to the formula employed on contracts and agreements from 143/2 BCE (SE 170), after Judaea obtained a large measure of autonomy from the Seleucids (1 Macc. 13.41-42; Josephus, *AJ* 13.213). We are told that these documents were issued with the authority of "Simon, the great high priest, general and leader of the Jews".

(a)

(b)

Ill. 7.15 (a) Rose with buds on Rhodes AR diobol = 1/3 drachm (10 mm, 0.8 gm); c. 188-84 BCE. *SNG Keckman* 1, no. 699; *HGC* 6, no. 1465. CNG Electronic Auction 289 (24 October 2012), lot 130; courtesy of the Classical Numismatic Group Inc.; (b) Rose with buds on Rhodian amphora stamp from Jerusalem inscribed with the Greek name 'Aristokleus'. PEF Archives, Object 1048; courtesy of the Palestine Exploration Fund. London. This is one of numerous stamped Rhodian amphora handles that have been found in Jerusalem.

Table 7.2. Size and weight relationships of the coins issued by John *Hyrcanus* I and their possible denominational values

Coins of John *Hyrcanus* I (134-104 BCE)	Coin weight, average and range: sample size shown in brackets	Coin diameter, average and range	Possible denominational value, per *SC* II.2, table on p. 52 (see Tables 5.1 and 7.1, above)
TJC type H	3.7 ± 0.3 gm (2) 3.4-4.0 gm	17 mm 16-18 mm	2 prutot (= C; dichalkon)
TJC types A, B, D, E, F, G, I	1.92 ± 0.01 gm (599) 1.12-3.06 gm	14 mm 13-15 mm	1 prutah (= D; chalkon)
TJC types C, J	0.9 ± 0.1 gm (10) 0.6-1.1 gm	11 mm 10-12 mm	½ prutah (= E; hemichalkon)

The palaeo-Hebrew script on the early Hasmonaean coins bears close similarities with that found on scrolls from the Dead Sea which are dated to about the same period (see example shown in Ill. 7.16). Within a few decades, this classical Hebrew script, which had a pedigree stretching back to the period of the pre-Exilic period, would become outmoded within the next century and replaced by replaced by the square Hebrew script that remains in regular use.

Ido Noy (2012) has suggested that the motif of facing cornucopias and pomegranate on the reverse of *Hyrcanus'* prutot symbolises the sweet fruits of Maccabean victory. This metaphor is given expression in 1 Macc. 14.8-13 when describing the peace and prosperity won by the sword during the rule of his father, Simon, but it could equally well describe John *Hyrcanus* I's own term of office:

> "They farmed their land in peace, and the land produced its crops, and the trees in the plains their fruit. Old men sat in the streets, talking together of their blessings; and the young men dressed themselves in splendid military style. Simon supplied the towns with food in plenty and equipped them with weapons for defence. His renown reached the ends of the earth. He restored peace to the land, and there were great rejoicings throughout Israel. Each man sat under his own vine and under his own fig tree. The enemies left the land and the enemy kings were crushed in those days".

Palaeo-Hebrew Script on Hasmonaean Coins and Dead Sea Scrolls

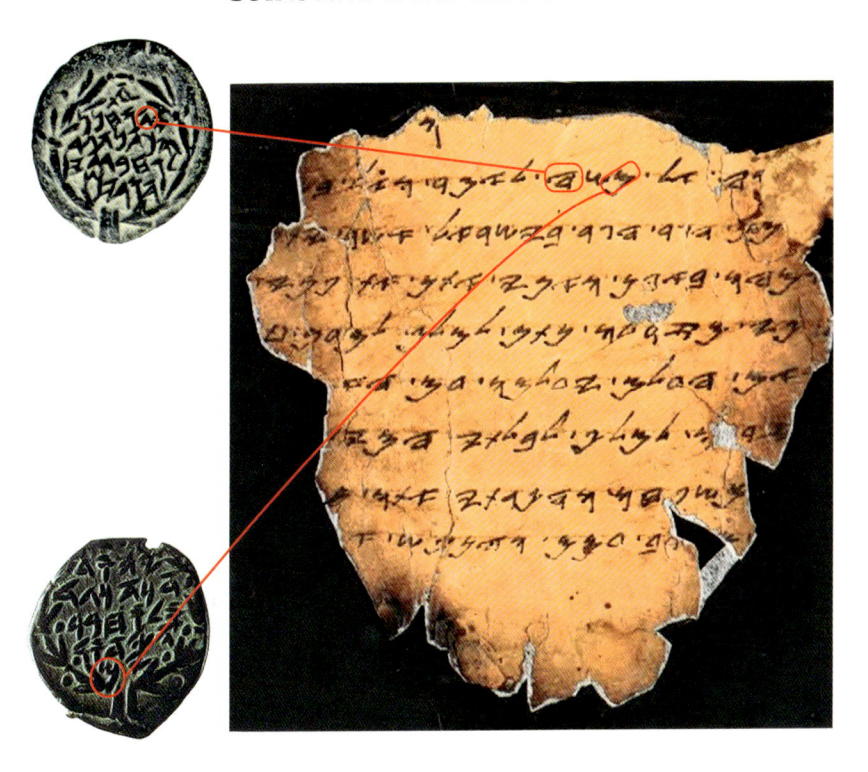

Ill. 7.16. The palaeo-Hebrew manuscript of Levi from Cave 11 at Qumran, fragment 4 (11Q paleoLev, fr. 4), showing the similarity of the script with that on prutot (chalkoi) of John *Hyrcanus* I and Judah Aristobulus I. The two letters indicated are the H and M in the name MŠH ("Moshe" or "Moses") on the scroll.

119

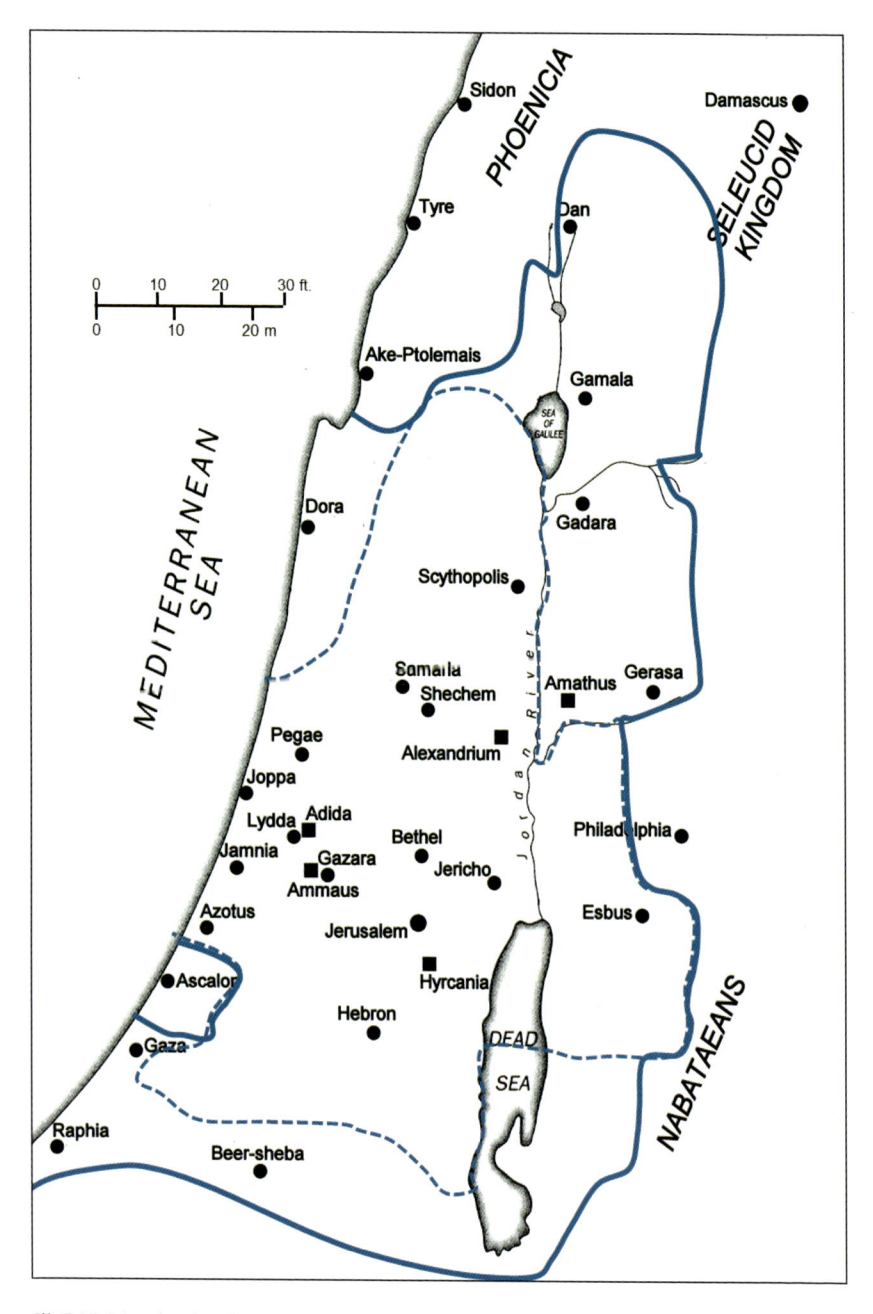

Ill. 7.17. Map showing the expansion Judaea from the rule of John *Hyrcanus* I to Alexander Jannaeus (104-76 BCE).

---- The Hasmonaean state at the death of John *Hyrcanus* I
—— The Hasmonaean state at the death of Alexander Jannaeus.

120   ANTIOCH AND JERUSALEM

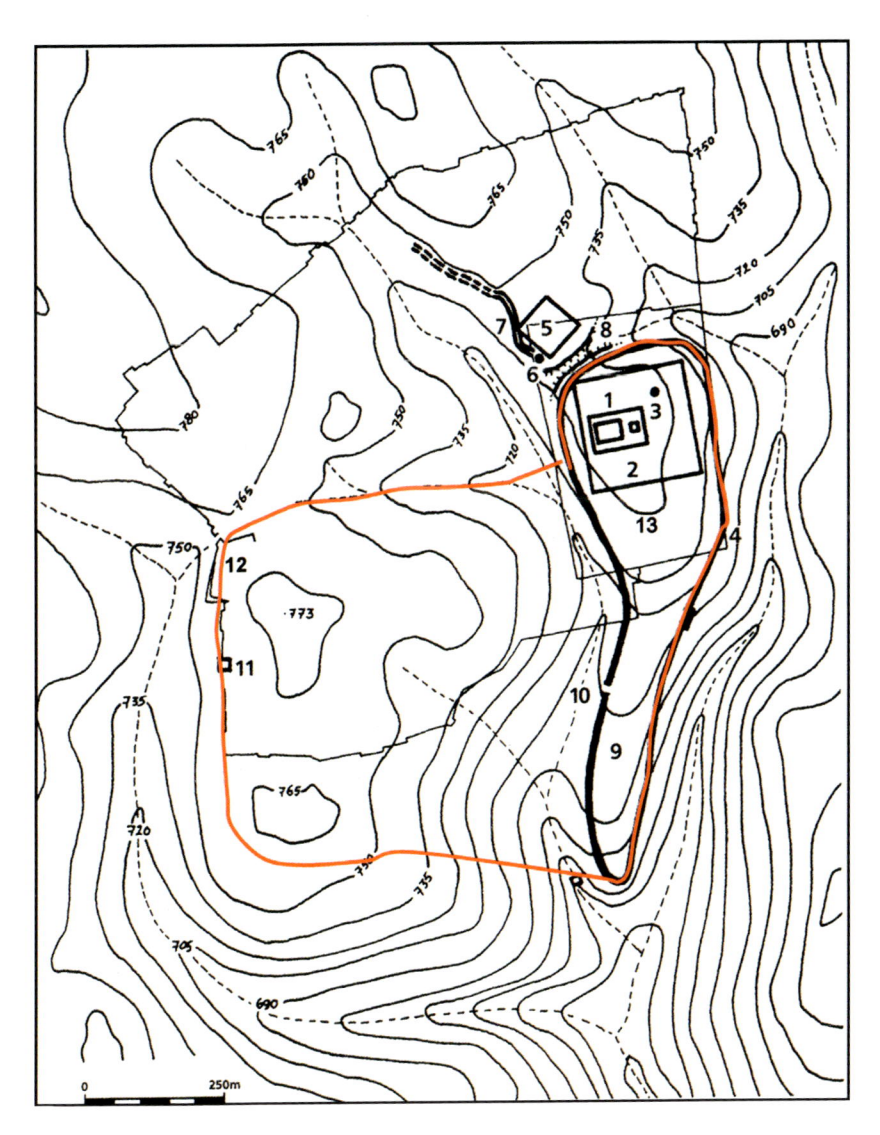

Ill.7.18. Map of Jerusalem showing the Hasmonaean city within its circuit of walls (indicated by a solid red line), in relation to the Ottoman Old City walls (indicated by a thin solid black line, enclosing an approximate square area). The topographical contours are given in metres.

Key to the numbers on the map: 1. Temple Sanctuary and altar; 2. Sanctified precinct of the Temple Mount; 3. Cistern; 4. Joint in the eastern wall of the Temple Mount where the Herodian (late 1st century BCE) extension, abuts on the earlier, coarser masonry of the Hasmonean perimeter of Jerusalem; 5. Suggested location of the Hasmonaean fortress of Jerusalem (*baris* in Greek; *birah* in Hebrew); 6. Cistern; 7. Conduit and rock-hewn passage to cistern (6); 8. Fosse (ditch); 9. Lower city (Ophel), where large numbers of wine amphora handles with Rhodian stamps have been found; 10. Remains of fortifications and gate; 11. Small fortified tower; 12. Surviving section of the Hasmonaean western wall of Jerusalem with a large Herodian tower, probably the one known as Hippicus in antiquity; 13. Possible site of the Seleucid *Akra*.

Ill. 7.19. Eastern wall of the Temple Mount, showing the lower courses of pre-Herodian masonry in the foreground – possibly part of the wall rebuilt by Jonathan *Apphus*, mentioned in 1 Macc. 12.37, and smoother Herodian stonework continuing to the south-east corner (no. 4 on the map of Jerusalem). Photograph courtesy of Professor Shimon Gibson.

Ill. 7.20. Surviving section of the Hasmonaean western wall of Jerusalem terminating in an imposing Herodian tower, probably the one called Hippicus in Josephus with its massive ashlar blocks, seen on the left (no. 12 on the map of Jerusalem). Photograph courtesy of Professor Shimon Gibson.

CHAPTER 8.

THE EXTINCTION OF THE SELEUCID KINGDOM AND SUBSEQUENT DEVELOPMENTS

A reduced rump of the Seleucid kingdom continued to linger for a few more years, if only because its neighbours considered it as a useful buffer between them. One by one, the more prosperous coastal cities shed their allegiance to the Seleucid monarchy. Proclaiming their autonomy, they replaced the monarch's bust on their coinage with the turreted head of Tyche, the tutelary deity that governed the fortune and prosperity of the metropolis, or a local deity, such as Melkart (literally the 'king of the city') venerated at Tyre. This contraction in the reach of Seleucid authority provided favourable conditions for the Hasmonaean kingdom to thrive and expand.

In the conflict in Anatolia between Mithradates VI of Pontus and General Lucius Cornelius Sulla of Rome (88-84 BCE), the Seleucids were largely left alone by both major combatants. Mithradates' ambitious son-in-law, Tigranes the Great, king of Armenia, however, saw the opportunity for expansion provided by the constant civil strife in the Seleucid kingdom to the south. In about 73/2 BCE, he invaded Syria and soon established his rule over that country. According to Josephus [*BJ* 1.116; *AJ* 13.419-20], Tigranes besieged Ake-Ptolemais in 70/69 BCE, during the reign of Alexandra Salome (76/5-67/6 BCE), and she sent envoys bearing gifts to appease him.

Ill. 8.1. Tyre. AR shekel/ tetradrachm (28 mm; 14.28 gm). Dated to year 11 of the city's era (116/5 BCE). Laureate bust of the city deity, Melkart / Eagle standing on a prow, palm on its right wing; AI (date) and a club to the left; letter 'bet' between the legs, monogram to the right. The Greek inscription reads ΤΥΡΟΥ ΙΕΡΑΣ ΚΑΙ ΑΣΥΛΟΥ, "of the holy and inviolable Tyre". *BMC Phoenicia*, p. 236, no. 71; *DCA*, no. 919.

Ill. 8.2. Sidon. Æ tetrachalkon (21.5mm; 6.7 gm). Dated CY 34 (78/7 BCE). Jugate busts of Tyche, veiled and turreted, and Zeus / Phoenician pentekonter; inscription reads L ΔΛ (date) and ΣΙΔΩΝΟΣ ΘΕΑΣ, "of the goddess of Sidon", above, and LṢDNM, "of the Sidonians" (in Phoenician), below. *BMC Phoenicia*, p. 164, no. 137; *HGC* 10, no. 283; *DCA*, no. 894.

For a succinct biography of Tigranes II and the relevant ancient sources, see 'Tigran II' in *Encyclopaedia Iranica* (http://www.iranicaonline.org/articles/tigran-ii).

Following the Roman general Lucullus' defeats of Mithradates VI and Tigranes in 69 BCE, a small Seleucid kingdom in Syria lingered under Antiochus XIII *Asiaticus* (1st reign 69/8-67/6 BCE, second reign 65 - 64 BCE*)*. Even now, civil wars continued, as another Seleucid, Philip II, challenged Antiochus. After the

Ill. 8.3. Arados. AR tetradrachm (28 mm; 15.33 gm). Dated to year 142 of the city's era (118/117 BCE). Turreted, veiled and draped bust of Tyche / Nike, holding an aphlaston and palm frond; behind, downwards, ΑΡΑΔΙΩΝ ("of Arados"); before, BMP (date) / Λ (Phoenician 'gimel') / ΔΝ; all set within an olive wreath border. *BMC Phoenicia*, p. 25, no. 199; *Duyrat* nos. 3161-64; *HGC* 10, no. 72.

Ill. 8.4. Seleucia Pieria. AR tetradrachm (29 mm; 14.85 gm). Autonomous issue, dated to year 10 of the city's era (99/98 BCE). Turreted, veiled and draped bust of Tyche / Filleted thunderbolt on a throne: I (date), below, A to the lower left; set within a wreath border. The Greek inscription reads ΣΕΛΕΥΚΕΩΝ ΤΗΣ ΙΕΡΑΣ / ΚΑΙ [Α]ΥΤΟΝΟΜΟΥ, "of Seleucia the holy and autonomous (city)". *HGC* 9, no. 1382; *DCA* 697 (CY 10 = 99/98 BCE).

According to a tradition reported by Appian of Alexandria, when Seleucus Nicator was about to build Seleucia Pieria, there was a portent of thunder, which caused Seleucus to consecrate a cult to thunder there, which continued into Appian's own time [Appian, *Syriaca* 58].

Ill. 8.5. Tigranes II of Armenia (95-56 BCE). AR tetradrachm (27 mm; 15.37 gm). Antioch mint. Struck 70-69 BCE. Head of Tigranes, diademed and draped, wearing a tiara decorated with a star between two eagles / Tyche of Antioch seated on a rock, holding a palm branch; below her feet the river god Orontes swimming; monograph in the inner right field; all within a wreath. The Greek inscription reads ΒΑΣΙΛΕΩΣ ΤΙΓΡΑΝΟΥ, "of King Tigranes". *CAA* 34.

The Tyche ensemble refers to a famous bronze sculpture in Antioch by Eutychides of Sicyon, a pupil of Lysippus, which was commissioned by Seleucus I Nicator [Pausanias, *Description of Greece* 6.2, 4; Malalas, *Chronographia*, 9.276.9]. This sculptural group is considered to have been groundbreaking because the two figures were set at right angles to one another, inviting viewing from all directions. It was also the first major artwork to feature Tyche as a city goddess wearing a mural crown. A Roman copy of this sculpture in marble is preserved in the Vatican Museum. The choice of the Tyche sculpture on this and other coins minted during or after Tigranes' occupation of Syria, highlights his pride in capturing Antioch, an illustrious city and one of the principal capitals of the Hellenistic world.

Ill. 8.6. Tigranes II of Armenia (95-56 BCE). Æ obol (23 mm ;11.23 gm). Armenian mint. Struck 70-66 BCE. Head of Tigranes II wearing an Armenian tiara / Tyche of Antioch seated on a rock, holding a palm branch; the river-god Orontes swimming below her feet. The Greek inscription is intended to read ΤΙΓΡΑΝΟΣ ΒΑΣΙΛΕΩΣ ΒΑΣΙΛΕΩ[Ν], "of Tigranes, King of Kings". Depeyrot, *Armenia*, p. 141, no. 24 (var.).

The bronze coin of Tigranes II from Armenia has a number of interesting features, including:

- The crude Greek inscription. The words ΤΙΓΡΑΝΟΣ ΒΑΣΙΛΕΩΣ are written back-to-front and upside-down to one another, and ΒΑΣΙΛΕΩ[Ν] is written incorrectly and in reverse, symptomatic of lack of fluency in Greek among celators in Armenia at that time. The title 'King of Kings' reminds us of Armenia's powerful eastern neighbour, Persia/Parthia, where this formula was habitually used for the royal title.

- The naiveté of both images illustrates the lack of artistic sophistication in 1st century BCE Armenia, as compared with artistic standards in Antioch and other Hellenistic centres.

Roman conquest of Pontus, the Romans became increasingly alarmed at the ongoing instability of Seleucid Syria. After Mithradates' final defeat by Gnaeus Pompeius Magnus (Pompey), in 64 BCE he marched into Syria, deposed the king, Antiochus XIII, and made that country a Roman province. The last scion of Antiochus VIII to rule in Syria, Philip II Philoromaios ("the friend of the Romans"), nicknamed *Barypous* ("heavy-footed"), was left as titular ruler in Cilicia until his death in c. 57/56 BCE. In 63 BCE, Pompey advanced from Syria towards the south, in order to establish the Roman supremacy in Phoenicia, Coele-Syria, and Palestine. At the time, Judaea was in the throes of the civil war between the Hasmonaean brothers, Hyrcanus II and Aristobulus II. Both sides bribed Pompey for his support, and a picked delegation of Pharisees appeared before him in support of Hyrcanus. Pompey decided to back Hyrcanus, and their joint army of Romans and Jews besieged Jerusalem for three months, after which it was taken from Aristobulus.

By the end of his eastern campaign, Pompey had embarked on a reorganisation of the Hellenistic East, creating new client kingdoms in the process.

> Shortly after the death of Queen Alexandra Salome in 67 BCE, discord between her eldest son and successor, Hyrcanus II, and his younger brother, Aristobulus II broke into the open. The latter defeated Hyrcanus in battle near Jericho, and usurped the offices of King and High Priest. Hyrcanus, initially clung on to Jerusalem, but fearing total defeat, fled to Petra, with the help of his able Idumaean aide, Antipater, the father of Herod the Great. There he joined forces with the Nabataean king, Aretas III, who agreed to support him after being promised the return of Nabataean towns that had been taken by the Hasmonaeans. Aretas advanced towards Jerusalem at the head of a 50,000 strong force, besieging the city for several months. Aristobulus bribed Marcus Aemilius Scaurus, deputy of the Roman general Gnaeus Pompeius Magnus (Pompey), to induce him to order Aretas to withdraw his army, which then suffered a crushing defeat at the hands of Aristobulus on its way back to Nabataea. Fighting between the Hasmonaean factions intensified, precipitating the direct intervention of Pompey in the internal Judaean quarrel [Josephus, *BJ* 1.120-130; *AJ* 14.4-33].

The bribe provided by Aristobulus II was the golden vine from the porch of the Temple, valued at 500 talents of silver (or 500 x 30 kg = 15 tonnes), which Pompey readily accepted. However, he soon tired of Aristobulus and switched his support to Hyrcanus. He marched on Jerusalem in 63 BCE, stormed the Holy City after a three month siege and deposed Aristobulus [Josephus, *BJ* 1.131-151; *AJ* 14.34-71].

Pompey appointed Hyrcanus II as Rome's client, with the title of *Ethnarches*, which served to emphasise the curtailment of the Hasmonaean monarchy [Josephus, *AJ* 20.244]. On capturing Jerusalem, Pompey entered the Temple and peered into the Holy of Holies, satisfying his curiosity about the Jews having no image of God in their inner Sanctum, but left it untouched [Josephus, *BJ* 1.152; *AJ* 14.72].

Coins Commemorating the Campaigns of Pompey's Forces in Judaea and Nabataea

During the reign of Aretas III (87-62 BCE), the Nabataean kingdom expanded to cover what is now northern area of Jordan and southern Syria, including Damascus, and reached its greatest territorial extent. In affirmation that Nabataea was now a serious political player in the Hellenistic world, Aretas styled himself "Philhellene" and struck the first silver Nabataean coins in Hellenic style with Greek inscriptions. Nabataean rule of Damascus was interrupted in 72 BCE by a successful siege led by the Armenian king, Tigranes II. Armenian rule of the city ended in 69 BCE when Tigranes' forces were pulled out to deal with a Roman attack on the Armenian capital, Tigranocerta (Tigranakert in Armenian), allowing Aretas to re-take Damascus. Despite the compliance of Aretas to the ultimatum of Aemilius Scaurus, one of Pompey's deputies, to withdraw his army from Judaea, in 62 BCE, Scaurus proceeded to launch a military expedition to Nabataea. It was called off when Aretas agreed to pay a tribute of 300 talents of silver (to Scaurus himself, each talent equal to roughly 30 kg of silver, worth a total of roughly $5 million in terms of today's purchasing power), a deal struck by Antipater, Hyrcanus' chief minister [Josephus, *AJ* 14.80-81; Bowersock 1983, 31-35]

Antioch remained the principal city of the eastern Mediterranean, alongside Alexandria, although both had waned in wealth and stature as Rome's power and prestige became pre-eminent and the Hellenistic kingdoms, of which these cities had been illustrious capitals, were snuffed out. The depths to which Antioch had sunk culturally is evident when one examines the highly stylised imagery on the coinage of this late period, exemplified by the tetradrachms struck under the authority of Aulus Gabinius (see Ill. 8.9). The naïve and rather formulaic style of the seated Zeus Nicephorus on this coin is in striking contrast with the highly

Ill. 8.7. AR denarius (18 mm; 4.13 gm) struck in 58 BCE in the names of M. Aemilius Scaurus, the deputy of Pompey on his eastern campaign, and P. Plautius Hypsaeus. Camel; in front, the supplicant Nabataean king, Aretas III (87-62 BCE), holding the reins and an olive branch. In exergue, REX ARETAS. The Latin inscription reads: M SCAVR / AED CVR / EX - S C / Jupiter brandishing a thunderbolt in a quadriga, with a scorpion in front. The Latin inscription reads: P HVPSAE / AED CVR / C HVPSAE COS / PREIVE and CAPTV behind the chariot. Crawford no. 422/1b; Harlan 1995, 66-72 (M. Aermilius Scaurus), 73-77 (P. Plautus Hypsaeus).

naturalistic rendering of the same subject on the tetradrachm of Seleucus Nicator with which this survey of Seleucid coinage commenced.

Julius Caesar, who succeeded Pompey as supreme Roman commander in 48 BCE, visited Antioch the following year, and confirmed its civic freedom. A great temple to Jupiter Capitolinus rose up on Mount Silpius, above the city, probably an initiative of Octavian (later awarded the title Augustus), whose cause the city had espoused. As part of the Augustan programme of civic and cultural regeneration throughout his empire, a forum of Roman type was laid out at the behest of Marcus Agrippa, while Herod the Great contributed a long colonnaded thoroughfare. Under Augustus, the Seleucid era was dropped in favour of the Actian one, severing a conspicuous link with the Hellenistic dynasty, and images of favourite Seleucid deities, notably Zeus Nicephorus and Apollo Delphius, were dropped in favour of civic subjects, such as the Tyche of Antioch.

Ill. 8.8. AR denarius (17 mm; 4.09 gm) struck in 55 BCE in the name of Curule Aedile, Aulus Plautius*. Head of Cybele wearing a mural crown, a distinction shared with Tyche and an attribute of their overlapping role as protectors of cities; before, A·PLAVTIVS downwards; behind, AED·CVR·S·C / Camel; in front, the supplicant Hasmonaean ruler and Jewish High Priest, Aristobulus II, holding reins in left hand and olive branch in r. hand. In exergue, BACCHIVS; before IVDAEVS, upwards. Crawford no. 431/1.

Aulus Plautius had served in Pompey's eastern campaign. The curious designation "Bacchius Iudaeus" (literally "Bacchic Jew") can be explained as follows: In an attempt to bribe Pompey and gain favour over his brother and rival, Hyrcanus II, Aristobulus II sent him the magnificent gold grape vine, which had adorned the vestibule of the Temple in Jerusalem, as a bribe. This vine, which was worth 500 talents, was paraded in Pompey's triumphal procession, where Aristobulus was led in triumph [Pliny, *Naturalis historia* 37.14; Plutarch, *Vitae Parallelae, Pompeius* 45]. It was then displayed in the temple of Jupiter Capitolinus, where it was noted together with the name of its donor by the historian, Strabo [Josephus, *AJ* 14.34-36]. Tacitus specifically ascribes the notion of the Jews worshipping Dionysus to the "golden vine that was found in their temple" [Tacitus, *Historiae* 5.5, 5]. By the year that this coin was struck, both Aristobulus II and Hyrcanus II, had submitted to Roman authority, and been stripped of most of their own temporal powers, leaving the surviving Hyrcanus with little more than his high priesthood, so that it would have been justified, when portraying the submission of Judaea to Pompey on a coin a decade later, to omit the name of either Hasmonaean brother and their now defunct sovereign title. See Crawford 431/1; Sydenham 932; B. *Plautia* 13; see Jacobson 2007a.

*A. Plautius was perhaps of a praetorian family, a tribune in 56 BCE, who pressed Pompey's claim on the Egyptian command by presenting documentation from Ptolemy Auletes. He turns up in the Pompeian forces in 49 BCE [Dio 39.16, 2; Cicero, *Epistulae ad Familiares* 13.29, 4]. Pompeian connections with the Plautii were manifold. In addition to Plautius Hypsaeus, there was the Plautius who sponsored an agrarian law for Pompey's veterans in 70. Yet another Plautius or Plotius was an officer for Pompey in the pirate war [Appian, *Mithridateios* 95; Florus 1.41, 9]. He is often identified with the A. Plautius who was a tribune of 56. More likely, he is C. Plotius, mentioned in 59 as a senator and former legate in Asia [Cicero, *Pro Flacco* 50]. See Harlan 1995, xvi and 115-18 (A. Plautius); Gruen 1974, 108 and n. 65 (cf. p. 107 and n. 62, re P. Plautius Hypsaeus).

Ill. 8.9. Antioch, Struck under Aulus Gabinius, Roman Proconsul, 57-55 BCE. AR tetradrachm (26 mm; 15.41 gm), imitating issue of Philip I Philadelphus. Diademed head of Philip I / Zeus seated, holding a Nike offering a wreath in his right hand and a sceptre in his left; AYΓB monogram = Au(lus) G(a)b(inius) in inner left field; all set within an olive wreath border. The Greek inscription reads [B]ΑΣΙΛΕΩΣ [Φ]ΙΛΙΠΠΟΥ (right side) ΕΠΙΦΑΝΟΥΣ ΦΙΛΑΔΕΛΦΟ[Υ] (left side), "of King Philip *Ephiphanes Philadelphus* (the brother lover made manifest)". *SC* no. 2489; *RPC* I no. 4124.

In 57 BCE, Aulus Gabinius, the Roman general serving Pompey, was sent as Proconsul to Syria. On his arrival, he confirmed Hyrcanus II as High Priest at Jerusalem and suppressed revolts by Aristobulus II (who had escaped from captivity in Rome) and his son Alexander. Aristobulus was brought back to Rome an second time, but was released from imprisonment by Julius Caesar, after the latter had displaced Pompey from power. In 49 BCE, the partisans of Pompey captured and poisoned Aristobulus and had his son Alexander beheaded at Antioch [Josephus, *BJ* 1.160-185; *AJ* 14.82-126].

Pompey and Gabinius made important changes to the government of Judaea, paring down its territory by detaching the coastal towns and rebuilding several towns that had been ruined in the previous period of strife [Josephus, *BJ* 1.155-178; *AJ* 14.74-104].

Following his Roman predecessors, Caesar confirmed Hyrcanus II as High Priest and hereditary Ethnarch. During the tenure of Hyrcanus II, the power and stature of his Idumaean chief minister, Antipater grew apace. Both were quick to demonstrate their support for Julius Caesar and rallied the Jews of Egypt to his side. In appreciation, Antipater was awarded Roman citizenship and exemption from taxes by Caesar, who also returned Joppa (Iopé, Jaffa) and other towns that had been detached from Judaea by Pompey to Hasmonaean jurisdiction [Josephus, *BJ* 1.187-194; *AJ* 14.127-139].

After Caesar's murder in 44 BCE, Hyrcanus II and Antipater submitted to the 'liberator' Cassius Longinus, who took control of Syria, and they acceded to his demand for a contribution of 7,000 talents from Judaea to his coffers. Within a year, Antipater departed from the scene, having been poisoned by one of Hyrcanus' butlers at the behest of a hostile Judaean or Idumaean commander, one Malichus, and quite possibly with the connivance of Hyrcanus. The defeat of Brutus and Cassius at Philippi in 43 BCE required Hyrcanus and the sons of Antipater to build bridges with Mark Antony. Of those sons, Phasael and Herod were appointed governors of the whole of Judaea, both with the title of tetrarch [Josephus, *BJ* 1.218-244; *AJ* 14.271-326].

In the spring of 40 BCE, the Parthians invaded the Levant and,

Ill. 8.10. Augustus (ruled 27 BCE -14 CE). AR tetradrachm (27 mm; 15.17 gm); dated to year 27 of the Actian Era (5/4 BCE). Antioch mint. Laureate head of Augustus, with inscription ΚΑΙΣΑΡΟΣ ΣΕΒΑΣΤΟΥ = Caesar Sebastos (Augustus) / Tyche seated on a rock right, holding palm branch; river-god Orontes swimming to right below, with inscription ΕΤΟΥΣ ΖΚ ΝΙΚΗΣ, "year 27 of the victory (at Actium)"; two monograms and IB in right field. *RPC* I no. 4152.

Compare the rendering of this sculptural ensemble on this coin with that on the coins of Tigranes II illustrated earlier (Ills. 8.5 and 8.6).

Fig. 8.11. Mattathiah Antigonus (40-37 BCE). Æ octochalkon (25 mm, 15.4 gm). Jerusalem mint. Two conjoined, facing cornucopias; surrounding inscription in palaeo-Hebrew: MTTYH KHN GDL ḤBR ..., "Mattathiah (Matthew), High Priest, (and) ḥever ..." and N' between the horns (apparently retrograde AN for "Antigonus") / Ivy wreath tied with ribbons; surrounding Greek inscription: ΒΑC[ΙΛΕΩC ΑΝΤ]ΙΓ(Ο)ΝΟΥ, "of King Antigonus". *TJC* no. 36d.

after spirited resistance led by Phasael and Herod, they occupied Judaea. They replaced Hyrcanus II as titular ruler of Judaea by a surviving son of Aristobulus II, Mattathiah (Mattathias) Antigonus, who enjoyed considerable support among the Jewish population. Hyrcanus and Phasael were captured and handed over to Antigonus. Herod managed to escape from Jerusalem and fled to Petra in Nabataea, where he received a frosty reception, so he proceeded to Alexandria and onwards to Rome. Antigonus mutilated Hyrcanus, by severing his ears, so as to make him unfit for the office of the high priesthood. Phasael committed suicide during his incarceration while Hyrcanus was taken into custody in Parthia [Josephus, *BJ* 1.248-281; *AJ* 14.330-378].

Antigonus remained at the helm of Judaea for almost three years. He emulated his grandfather Alexander Jannaeus in using the royal title, as attested by the Greek inscriptions on his coins. The majority of Antigonus' coins bear the same motifs as those employed on issues of John *Hyrcanus* I, in particular cornucopias and wreaths, but at the end of his reign, he issued chalkoi displaying distinctive appurtenances from the Jerusalem Temple, the Menorah and Table of the Showbread.

Herod's visit to Rome in 40 BCE was timely and productive. When he arrived, Herod was presented to the Senate and was formally appointed king at the recommendation of Mark

Antony and Octavian Caesar (the future Augustus). He was provided with military and financial aid to gain his throne at the expense of Antigonus. The following year, he sailed to Ptolemais, the Parthians having evacuated Syria and Judaea under pressure from Roman legions. With Roman support, Herod succeeded in defeating Antigonus' forces and gained possession of Judaea and its capital Jerusalem, after a five month siege, in 37 BCE. Antigonus surrendered to the Roman governor of Syria, C. Sosius when Jerusalem fell. Sosius mocked him, calling him Antigone, as though he were a woman. When Antony "heard that the [Jewish] nation was rebellious and had remained loyal to Antigonus out of hatred for Herod, he decided to behead him in Antioch". In such an ignominious manner did the Hasmonaean dynasty, begun by the glorious Maccabees, meet its terrible end. It had outlasted its Seleucid protagonists by just over six decades [Josephus, *BJ* 1.282-357; *AJ* 14.379-491; 15.8-9].

Fig. 8.12. Mattathiah Antigonus. Æ tetrachalkon (20 mm, 7.7 gm). Jerusalem mint. Cornucopia tied with a ribbon; surrounding inscription in palaeo-Hebrew: MTTYH HKHN HG[D], "Mattathiah, the High Priest" / Greek inscription on three lines: [BA]CIΛE(ΩC)/[AN]TIΓO/NOY, "of King Antigonus" within a wreath, tied at the left. *TJC* no. 37b.

Fig. 8.13. Mattathiah Antigonus. Æ chalkon (12 mm, 1.8 gm). Jerusalem mint. Ear of barley between two conjoined, facing cornucopias adorned with ribbons / Retrograde palaeo-Hebrew inscription MTT/YH, "Mattathiah" within wreath; *TJC* no. 40.

APPENDIX.

GREEK, ROMAN AND JEWISH SOURCES CITED

For more detailed information about Greek and Roman sources the *Oxford Classical Dictionary* (ed. Hornblower, Spawnforth and Eidinow, 4th edn., 2012) can be recommended. It offers the convenience that entries are listed alphabetically. Schürer (1973-87) and the *Encyclopedia Judaica* (2nd edn., 2006) can be recommended for background on the biblical and post-biblical Jewish works cited (Nehemiah, Daniel, 1 and 2 Maccabees, Scroll of [Megillat] Ta'anit and the Babylonian Talmud). Josephus is generally included in both categories – Jewish and Greek authors.

Greek and Roman Sources:

Source	Dates	Summary Information
Appian of Alexandria	End of 1st century-160s CE	Greek historian, who wrote mainly during the reign of Antoninus Pius. Compiled a series of narratives in 24 books in Greek of Roman conquests up to the accession of Vespasian in 69 CE. Of these works, nine survive complete and portions of others as well. Among these is the *Syriaca*, or Syrian Wars.
Athenaeus	Late 2nd–early 3rd century CE	Greek rhetorician and grammarian from Naucratis in the Nile Delta. Of his several writings, the *Deipnosophistae* ("Banquet of the Learned") mostly survives; books 1-2 and parts of 3, 11 and 15 only survive in epitome. It is a treasure trove of passages from other ancient works, otherwise mostly lost, representing nearly 2,500 different compositions and 800 authors. It is mostly concerned with dining, but there are some interesting details about the luxury enjoyed by Hellenistic monarchs and associated biographical information.

Source	Dates	Summary Information
(Marcus Tullius) Cicero	106-43 BCE	Outstanding Roman orator, lawyer, statesman and prolific author. His writings, many of which survive, rank among the most influential in European culture, and one of our main sources on late Roman Republican history and culture. Although a staunch Republican, he stayed out of the conspiracy to assassinate Julius Caesar, but developed hostility to Mark Antony, attacking him in speeches. He was proscribed as an enemy of the state by the Second Triumvirate and killed.
(Cassius) Dio	c.164 – c.235 CE	Senator born in Nicaea, Bithynia, and author of a "History of Rome" to 229 CE in 80 books in Greek. Of these, only books 36-54 covering the years 68-10 BCE survive complete, some others in part or epitome. The rest is known from summary descriptions of later Byzantine historians. He is an important source but not always unreliable.
Diodorus Siculus	Flourished 60-30 BCE	Greek historian from Sicily, who compiled a world history to 60 BCE, which he titled *Bibliotheca historica* ("Historical Library"). It is centred on Rome, and comprised 40 books, 15 of which survive complete, others in fragments. He drew uncritically on the works of earlier authors, but is useful in conveying their material, which is otherwise mostly lost.

Source	Dates	Summary Information
Eusebius	c.260-340 CE	Bishop of Caesarea and Greek-Christian author. His most important work is the *Ecclesiastical History*, the first of its kind. It is divided into 10 books and constitutes an important source on the history of Christianity from its origins to 324 CE. His *Preparatio evangelica* ("Preparation for the Gospel") preserves portions of Hellenistic Jewish writings written in Greek – histories, poetry and even a large portion of a tragic play – which do not survive elsewhere. Eusebius' *Chronicon* ("Chronicle") preserves some valuable chronological information on the Seleucids from Porphyry of Tyre, a 3rd century CE scholar and philosopher (Eusebius, *Chronicon* 1, pp. 247-263). Eusebius' *Onomasticon* is a valuable compendium of places mentioned in the Bible, with his identification of their location.
(Lucius Annaeus/ Julius) Florus	Flourished in the mid-2nd century CE	Roman historian who wrote an abridgement (epitome) in Latin of "all the wars through 700 years", with emphasis given to the wars waged up to the reign of Augustus. For this work, the author drew on the writings of others, including Livy, Sallust and Caesar, although is sometimes at variance with them.

Source	Dates	Summary Information
(Flavius) Josephus	37/8- c. 100 CE	Jewish historian, of priestly descent, commander from 66-67 CE of the combined Jewish rebel forces in Galilee and author of the following four works, all extant in Greek: (a) *Bellum Judaicum* (*BJ*; in 7 books) detailing the 1st Jewish Revolt from 66-73 CE as an eye-witness, and also the events leading up to it; (b) *Antiquitates Judaicae* (*AJ*; in 20 books) giving an account of Jewish history from the Creation up to 66 CE. The earlier books follow the biblical narrative, but the subsequent ones provide precious information about the period from the 4th century BCE to the outbreak of the war against Rome. It is a crucial source information about the Seleucid kingdom, and provides almost the only biographical data on the reigns of Demetrius III and Antiochus XII ; (c) *Vita*: mostly a rebuttal of the allegations of his detractor, Justus of Tiberias, claiming that he was complicit in instigating the rebellion; (d) *Contra Apionem* (in 2 books), the name given by Jerome, to a treatise about the antiquity of the Jews and answers to anti-Semitic slanders and falsehoods. He was captured at Jotapata and his life was spared after prophesying that Vespasian, the Roman commander, would become emperor.

Source	Dates	Summary Information
Justin (Marcus Junian[i]us Justinus) – for Pompeius Trogus	2nd or 3rd century CE, or even later.	Roman historian who wrote an abridgement in Latin of the history of the 1st century BCE Augustan historian, Pompeius Trogus, (the *Historiae Philippicae*), which is now lost. Trogus' history, in 44 books, focused on the history of Macedon and the Hellenistic kingdoms, and some important information about them is preserved in Justin's epitome. Trogus' *Prologi* ('Summaries") has survived separately intact.
Livy (Titus Livius)	59 BCE – 17 CE	Roman historian, born in Padua. Author of the monumental "History of Rome from its Foundation" (*Ab urbe condita libri*) down to 9 BCE in 142 books, of which only books 1-10, 21-45 survive complete (apart from books 41 and 43 which are incomplete). There are also epitomes of books 37-40 and 48-55 and short abstracts, or summaries (*Periochae*) for all the books, except 136 and 137. The last 22 books dealt with the events of his lifetime. He mostly relied on other historical works rather than original records and tended to be uncritical of his sources. While his Latin prose style is elegant, Livy's limited life experience is reflected in his unrealistic description of military matters and political institutions. He is also rather weak on social and economic conditions in Rome at various times.

Source	Dates	Summary Information
(John) Malalas	c.480-c.570 BCE	Christian Greek speaker from Antioch who moved to Constantinople in the mid-6th century CE. Author of a universal history in 18 books (the *Chronographia*, or "Chronicle of World History"), which breaks off in 563 CE. This work is regarded to have very limited value as a primary source, apart from his account of the period close to his own lifetime. It also includes some interesting snippets of information about the Seleucid kings.
Palatine Anthology	7th century BCE – c.600 CE	One of two surviving collections of poems in Greek from antiquity, mostly epigrams, named after the Palatine library in Heidelberg, where the single surviving manuscript of this anthology, dating from the 10th century, was found in 1606 (the other collection being the Planudean Anthology of the 14th century).
Pausanias	Flourished mid-2nd century CE	Greek travel writer. Author of a "Description of Greece", based on his own travels. His account and associated historical information seems to be mostly reliable, and therefore represents an invaluable record. His main interest is in places, buildings and objects of religious and historical importance, including works of art. He was less attracted to structures and objects later than 150 BCE. His itinerary excludes Aetolia and the Greek islands.

Source	Dates	Summary Information
Pliny the Elder (Gaius Plinius Secundus)	23/4-79 CE	Roman writer of natural history, born in Como, northern Italy. He spent his early adulthood in military service, mostly on the Rhine where he rubbed shoulders with the future emperor Titus. He then spent several years in legal advocacy, followed by administrative posts in Roman provinces. He was close to Vespasian and Titus, who appointed him commander of the fleet at Misenum (near Naples) in 79 CE. In August that year, he sailed to observe the eruption of Vesuvius, got too close and was suffocated by the fumes. Pliny had an enquiring mind, an insatiable curiosity, and was highly industrious. His greatest legacy is the *Naturalis historia* ("Natural History") in 37 books, dedicated to Titus. This work is encyclopaedic in scope, a mine of information about the art, natural history, mineralogy, medicines, geography, ethnology, and other subjects, as known at that time.

Source	Dates	Summary Information
Plutarch(os), or Lucius Mestrius Plutarchus	c. 46 – 120 CE	Greek historian, biographer essayist from Chaeronia, near Delphi, best known for his *Vitae parallelae* ("Parallel Lives") of eminent Greeks and Romans. He also wrote biographies of the Roman Emperors from Augustus to Vitellius, of which, only the Lives of Galba and Otho survive complete, while those of Tiberius and Nero are extant as fragments. His "Parallel Lives" are arranged in pairs to highlight their shared virtues and vices. There remain 23 pairs, each with one Greek Life and one Roman Life, as well as four unpaired single Lives, not all in their complete state. Several of the constituent biographies have not survived. Plutarch's other remaining works have been brought together in the *Moralia* ("Customs and Mores"), comprising essays and transcribed speeches.
Polybius	c.200– c.118 BCE	Greek historian from Megalopolis, who documented the Mediterranean world during Rome's rise to become its dominant power. A captive in Italy during his early adulthood, he became a close associate of the Scipio family, witnessing the destruction of Carthage in the company of Scipio Aemilianus, one of Rome's leading commanders. His major literary work is his "Histories" in 40 books, of which only the first five survive complete. For the rest, there are only excerpts and quotations by other writers. Polybius regarded the study of original documents and memoirs, as well as first-hand knowledge of events as of foremost importance, which makes the remains of his historical account, highly valuable. A major theme running through it is the important role played by fortune (*Tyche*) in the rise of Rome.

Source	Dates	Summary Information
Porphyry	c. 232/3 – c. 305 CE	Neoplatonic philosopher from Tyre. He was a prolific writer of philosophical works, but is best known for his cleverly argued critique of Christians and their beliefs (*Adversos Christianos*) in 15 books, now only known through the refutations presented by Church Fathers, including Eusebius and Jerome. His historical work, the *Chronica* is largely preserved in the *Chronicon* of Eusebius.
Strabo	c. 64 BCE – c.24 CE	Greek speaking geographer and historian from Amaseia, Pontus. His "Historical Notes" in 47 books is lost, apart from some quotations in works by other authors. His surviving *Geographia* in 17 books is the major source book on ancient geography and one of the most important surviving literary works of the Augustan age. In it he describes the physical geography of lands known to him, and provides sketches of their local history, economic activities and customs.

Source	Dates	Summary Information
(Publius?) Cornelius Tacitus	c. 56 –c. 118 CE	Roman historian, probably from southern Gaul. He was successful in Roman society, being appointed a senator under Vespasian (69-79 CE), marrying the daughter of the governor of Britain, Julius Agricola, and made governor of Asia in 112-113 CE. His major works are his *Historiae* ("Histories") and *Ab excessu divi Augusti* ("Annals"). The former covered the period 69-96 CE, but only the first four books covering the years 69-70 CE survive. These paint a vivid picture of upheavals associated with the 'Year of the Four Emperors', ending with Vespasian's triumph. The "Annals", which covered 14 – 68 CE, that is the Julio-Claudian emperors after Augustus, has parts of books 5 and 6 and all of 7-10 now missing and the last, book 16, breaks off before the death of Nero. His surviving writings show a historian with a penetrating insight into character and a critical approach, for the most part, to his subject matter.

Biblical and Post-Biblical Jewish Sources:

Source	Dates	Summary Information
Nehemiah	c. 400 BCE (for the memoir that forms the basis of this work)	Biblical book describing the efforts of Nehemiah to rebuild Jerusalem under Persian rule and carry out reforms among the restored Jewish inhabitants of the Holy city. He probably flourished in the second half of the 5th century BCE.
Daniel	c. 165 BCE	A Jewish apocalyptic work, divided into a series of stories in (chapters 1–6) in which the protagonist, Daniel, and his companions demonstrate the superiority of their God, followed by a series of visions described in chapters 7–12. The introductory and concluding sections are in Hebrew, the rest is composed in Aramaic. Chapters 10-12 show awareness of Antiochus IV's two campaigns in Egypt and his desecration of the Temple of Jerusalem, but not about his death.
1 Maccabees	Late 2nd century BCE (Hebrew original)	Work describing the struggle for Jewish independence from Seleucid rule chronologically, beginning with the oppressive measures taken by Antiochus IV Epiphanes with the support of the Jewish Hellenists, and ending with the death of Simon *Thassi*, the last of the Maccabee brothers. It was originally composed in Hebrew: the original Hebrew version is lost but this work survives in the Greek translation as part of the Septuagint version of the Bible. The book is regarded as canonical scripture by some Christian churches (but not the Protestant ones).

Source	Dates	Summary Information
2 Maccabees	Late 2nd century BCE	A work written in *koine* Greek about the epic struggle of the Maccabees, focusing on the Jewish revolt against Antiochus IV Epiphanes and concluding with the defeat of the Seleucid general Nicanor in 161 BCE by Judas Maccabeus, the hero of the book, covering much of the same ground as roughly the first half of 1 Maccabees. To this is added material, evidently Pharisaic in origin, including prayer for the dead and a resurrection on Judgment Day. It also includes a few apparently authentic historical documents. The author seems primarily interested in providing a theological interpretation of the events – stressing acts of divine intervention and punishment of the wicked – rather than a narrative chronicle. Indeed, some events are presented out of chronological order. Catholic and Orthodox Christians consider this work, which is part of the Septuagint Bible, to be canonical.
Scroll of Ta'anit (*Megillat Ta'anit*)	Second half of the 1st century CE; the Hebrew scholia added in c. 7th century CE	A calendar which enumerates 35 important days in Jewish history, which happened between the 2nd century BCE and the 1st century CE, in which joyful events occurred and on which fasting is not permitted. Most editions of this work contain two parts, the text proper, written in Aramaic and giving pity outlines, and scholia or commentaries on this text, written in Hebrew. It is divided into 12 sections, corresponding to the months of the year, starting with the notable events in Nisan, and ending with those of the 12th month, Adar.

Source	Dates	Summary Information
Tosefta	c. 220 – late 4th century CE	Tosefta, meaning "supplement", is regarded as an addition to the Mishnah. The Mishnah is the basic body of the Oral law of Judaism, divided into 63 Hebrew tractates, which was edited by Rabbi Judah ha-Nasi ("the Prince") in the early 3rd century. The Tosefta shares the same structure as the Mishnah. It is mainly written in Hebrew, with the remainder in Aramaic. It often attributes laws that are anonymous in the Mishnah to named rabbis.
Jerusalem Talmud	c. 220 - c. 400 CE	Compilation of Jewish Oral Law, as elaborated on the written Laws of Moses in the Bible. It consists of the Mishnah, in 63 Hebrew tractates, edited by Rabbi Judah ha-Nasi ("the Prince") in the early 3rd century and discussions on these in Aramaic by eminent rabbis, edited in Tiberias, Galilee, and surviving as 39 tractates.
Babylonian Talmud	c. 220 – c. 500 CE	Compilation of Jewish Oral Law, as elaborated on the written Laws of Moses in the Bible. It consists of the Mishnah and discussions of its contents in Aramaic by eminent rabbis, edited by Rabbis Ravina and Ashi in Babylonia. Only 36 of these tractates are extant.

BIBLIOGRAPHY

Scholarly biographies of the Seleucid kings and queens, together with comprehensive references to textual sources – both ancient and modern, are given in Grainger 1997 and *SC* 1 and 2. Briefer outlines with selected bibliographies are to be found on the Internet. Especially recommended are:

1. www.seleukidtraces.info/. *Seleukid Traces* is the initiative of Petr Veselý in the UK. It is a mine of quality information on the Seleucid dynasty, developed around a collection of coins acquired by that author.

2. http://www.seleukidempire.org/. *The Seleukid Empire*, a website of Oliver Hoover is presented as "an online sourcebook for the history, numismatics, epigraphy, art and archaeology of the Seleucid Empire".

3. www.livius.org/. *Livius* is a website devoted to Ancient History, which was set up and maintained by written and maintained by Jona Lendering, a historian in the Netherlands. It includes the following series of web features:

(a). www.livius.org/se-sg/seleucids/seleucid_kings.html, a short collection of biographies of the Seleucid monarchs.

(b). www.livius.org/cg-cm/chronicles/chron00.html, an online prepublication of I. Finkel and R.J. van der Spek, *Babylonian Chronicles of the Hellenistic Period* (= *BCHP*). Particularly relevant for the period covered by this book are cuneiform documents *BCHP*, nos. 13-18, which are informative about reigns of Antiochus III-V and Demetrius II.

(c). http://www.livius.org/di-dn/diaries/astronomical_diaries.html, the *Babylonian Astronomical Diaries*, which constitute another useful source bearing on Seleucid history. This series of cuneiform tablets record celestial phenomena and correlate these with important political events. Those that relate to the period of Seleucid rule are published in A. Sachs and H. Hunger, Vol. 2: *Diaries from 261 to 165 BCE* (1989) and Vol. 3: *Diaries from 164 to 61 BCE* (1996), Vienna: Austrian Academy of Sciences.

A useful starting point for exploring the Hasmonaean dynasty and the history of the period is the article 'Hasmonean dynasty' in Wikipedia, at http://en.wikipedia.org/wiki/Hasmonean_dynasty. It is liberally illustrated with pictures, maps and genealogical diagrams. There are hypertext links to other articles on individual Hasmonaean leaders and many other related topics. For ancient Jewish coin types (including those of the Hasmonaeans and earlier), see the *Menorah Coin Project* of the Israel Numismatic Society at http://menorahcoinproject.org.

BMC Phoenicia	Hill, G. F., 1910. *A Catalogue of the Greek Coins in the British Museum* 26: *The Greek Coins of Phoenicia*, London: Trustees of the British Museum.
CAA	Bedoukian. P. Z., 1978. *Coinage of the Artaxiads of Armenia*. London: Royal Numismatic Society.
Crawford	Crawford, M. H., 1974. *Roman Republican Coinage*, Cambridge: Cambridge University Press.
DCA	Cohen, E., 2011. *Dated Coins of Antiquity: A Comprehensive Catalogue of the Coins and How Their Numbers Came About*. Lancaster, PA: Classical Numismatic Group.
Depeyrot, *Armenia*	Mousheghian, A., and Depeyrot, G., 1999. *Hellenistic and Roman Armenian Coinage (1st c. BC - 1st c. AD)*. Moneta 15. Wettern.
Duyrat	Duyrat, F., 2005. *Arados Hellénistique: Étude historique et monétaire* (Bibliothèque archéologique et historique 173), Beirut: Institut français du Proche-Orient
Encyclopedia Judaica	*Encyclopedia Judaica* 2006, New York: Macmillan Reference USA, 22 vols.
HGC 6	Hoover, O. D., 2010. *Handbook of Coins of the Islands: Adriatic, Ionian, Thracian, Aegean, and Carpathian Seas (excluding Crete and Cyprus): Sixth to First Centuries B.C.* (The Handbook of Greek Coins, Vol. 6), Lancaster, PA / London: Classical Numismatic Group.
HGC 9	Hoover, O. D., 2009. *Handbook of Syrian Coins: Royal and Civic Issues: Fourth to First Centuries B.C.* (The Handbook of Greek Coins, Vol. 9), Lancaster, PA / London: Classical Numismatic Group.
IG²	*Inscriptiones Graecae, editio minor*, 1924- , Berlin: Walter de Gruyter.
IGLS 3.1	Jalabert, L., and Mouterde, R., (eds.), 1950. *Inscriptions grecques et latines de la Syrie* 3.1, *Région de l'Amanus. Antiochene, nos. 699-988* (Bibliothèque archéologique et historique 46), Paris: P. Geuthner.
Mørkholm, *Portraits*	Morkholm, O., 1979. 'The portrait coinage of Ptolemy V. The main series', in O. Morkholm and N. M. Waggoner (eds.), *Greek Numismatics and Archaeology: Essays in Honor of Margaret Thompson*, Wetteren: Cultura Press, 203-14.
Price	Price, M. J., 1991. *The Coinage in the Name of Alexander the Great and Philip Arrhidaeus: A British Museum Catalogue*, Zurich / London: Swiss Numismatic Society / British Museum Press.
RPC 1	Burnett, A., Amandry, M., and Ripollès, P., 1992. *Roman Provincial Coinage*, Vol. 1 (in 2 parts): *From*

	the *Death of Caesar to the Death of Vitellius (44 BC – AD 69)*, London: British Museum Press / Paris: Bibliothèque nationale de France..
SC 1	Houghton, A., and Lorber, C., 2002. *Seleucid Coins: A Comprehensive Catalogue*, *Part 1* (2 vols.): *Seleucus I through Antiochus III*, by New York / Lancaster, NY / London: American Numismatic Society / Classical Numismatic Group.
SC 2	Houghton, A., Lorber, C., and Hoover, O., 2008. *Seleucid Coins: A Comprehensive Catalogue, Part 2* (2 vols.): *Seleucus IV through Antiochus XIII*, New York / Lancaster, NY / London: American Numismatic Society / Classical Numismatic Group.
SNG Copenhagen 14	Schwabacher, W., and Breitenstein, N., (eds.), 1944. *Sylloge Nummorum Graecorum, The Royal Collection of Coins and Medals, Danish National Museum;* Vol. 14, *Attica –Aegina,* Copenhagen: Einar Munksgaard.
SNG France	Levante, E., 2001. *Sylloge Nummorum Graecorum, France 5; Départment des Monnaies, Médailles et Antiques, Mysie,* Paris: Bibliothèque Nationale de France / Numismatica Ars Classica.
SNG Israel 1	Houghton, A., and Spaer, A., 1998. *Sylloge Nummorum Graecorum, The Arnold Spaer Collection of Seleucid Coins,* London: Italo Vecchi
SNG Keckman 1	Westermark, U., and Ashton, R., (eds.), 1994. *Sylloge Nummorum Graecorum, Finland, The Erkki Keckman Collection in the Skopbank, Helsinki, Part 1: Karia,* Helsinki: The Finnish Society of Sciences and Letters.
Svoronos	Svoronos, J. N.,1904. *Ta Nomismata tou Kratous ton Ptolemaion (Ptolemaic Coinage)*, Athens: Sakellariou.
Sydenham	Sydenham, E. A., 1952, *The coinage of the Roman Republic*, rev. edn., ed. L. Forrer and C. A. Hersh, with indexes by G.C. Haines, London : Spink.
Thompson	Thompson. M., 1961. *The New Style Silver Coinage of Athens* (American Numismatic Society Numismatic Studies 10), New York: American Numismatic Society
Thompson *Lysimachus*	Thompson, M., 1968. 'The Mints of Lysimachus', in C. M. Kraay and G. K. Jenkins (eds.), *Essays in Greek Coinage Presented to Stanley Robinson*. Oxford: Clarendon Press.
TJC	Meshorer, Y., 2001. *A Treasury of Jewish Coins from the Persian Period to Bar Kokhba*, Nyack, NY: Amphora Books.

General References

Austin, M. M., 2006. *The Hellenistic World from Alexander to the Roman Conquest: A Selection of Ancient Sources in Translation* (2nd edn.), Cambridge: Cambridge University Press.

Bickerman, E., 1962. *From Ezra to the Last of the Maccabees: Foundations of Post-Biblical Judaism*, New York: Schocken.

Chamoux, F., 2003. *Hellenistic Civilization* (translated by M. Roussel), Malden, MA / Oxford: Blackwell Publishing.

Davies, W. D., and Finkelstein, L., (eds.), 1990. *The Cambridge History of Judaism*: vol. 2, *The Hellenistic Age*, Cambridge: Cambridge University Press.

Davis, N., and Kraay, C. M., 1973. *The Hellenistic Kingdoms: Portrait Coins and History*, London: Thames and Hudson.

Eckstein, A. M., 2008. *Rome Enters the Greek East: From Anarchy to Hierarchy in the Hellenistic Mediterranean, 230-170 BC*, Malden, MA / Oxford / Carlton, Victoria: Blackwell Publishing.

Feldman, L. H., 1993. *Jew and Gentile in the Ancient World: Attitudes and Interactions from Alexander to Justinian*, Princeton, NJ: Princeton University Press.

Grabbe, L. L., and Lipschits, O., (eds.), 2011. *Between East and West: The Transition from Persian to Greek Rule (ca. 400-200 BCE)* (Library of Second Temple Studies 75), London / New York: T. & T. Clark.

Grainger, J. D., 2012. *The Wars of the Maccabees: The Jewish Struggle for Freedom, 167-37 BC*, Barnsley: Pen & Sword Books.

Grainger, J. D., 1997. *A Seleukid Prosopography and Gazetteer* (Mnemosyne Suppl. 172), Leiden / New York / Köln: Brill.

Green, P., 1990. *From Alexander to Actium: The Historical Evolution of the Hellenistic Age*, Berkeley / Los Angeles: University of California Press.

Gruen, E., 1984. *The Hellenistic World and the Coming of Rome*, 2 vols. Berkeley / Los Angeles: University of California Press.

Habicht, C., 2006. *The Hellenistic Monarchies*, Ann Arbor: University of Michigan Press.

Hengel, M., 1974. *Judaism and Hellenism. Studies in Their Encounter in Palestine during the Early Hellenistic Period* (2 vols.; translated by J. Bowden), London: SCM Press.

Hendin, D., 2010. *Guide to Biblical Coins* (5th edn.), New York: Amphora.

Hornblower, S., Spawforth, A., and Eidinow, E., 2012. *The Oxford Classical Dictionary* (4th edn.), Oxford: Oxford University Press.

Levine, L. I., 2002. *Jerusalem: Portrait of the City in the Second Temple Period (538 B.C.E. – 70 C.E)*, Philadelphia, PA: Jewish Publication Society, 45-148.

Levine, L. I., 1998. *Judaism and Hellenism in Antiquity: Conflict or Confluence?*, Seattle / London: University of Washington Press.

Pearlman, M., 1973. *The Maccabees*, New York: Macmillan.

Schürer, E., 1973-87. *The History of the Jewish People in the Age of Jesus Christ (175 B.C. - A.D. 135)*, rev. and ed. by G. Vermes, F. Millar and M. Black, 4 vols., Edinburgh: T & T Clark.

Specialist References

Abramson, H., 1975. 'The Olympieion in Athens and its connections with Rome', *Journal of Social Science, Culture and Arts* (*CASCA*) 7, 1-25

Aperghis, G. G., 2004. *The Seleukid Royal Economy: The Finances and Financial Administration of the Seleukid Empire*, Cambridge: Cambridge University Press.

Bertrand, J. M., 1982. 'Sur l'inscription d'Hefzibah,' *Zeitschrift für Papyrologie und Epigraphik* 46, 167-74.

Bar-Kochva, B., 1989. *Judas Maccabaeus: The Jewish Struggle against the Seleucids*, Cambridge: Cambridge University Press.

Barag, D., and Qedar, S., 1980. 'The Beginning of Hasmonean Coinage', *Israel Numismatic Journal* 4, 8-21.

Bartlett, J. R., 2003. '1 Maccabees' and '2 Maccabees', in *Eerdmans Commentary on the Bible*, Grand Rapids, MI: Eerdmans, 807-850.

Baumgarten, A. I., 1996. 'Invented traditions of the Maccabaean era,' in H. Cancik, H. Lichtenberger and P. Schäfer (eds.), *Geschichte, Tradition, Reflexion: Festschrift fur Martin Hengel zum 70. Geburtstag*, Tübingen: J.C.B. Mohr, Vol.1, 197-210.

Bellinger, A. R., 1949. 'The end of the Seleucids', *Transactions of the Connecticut Academy of Arts and Sciences* 38, 51-102.

Berlin, A. A., 1997. 'Between large forces: Palestine in the Hellenistic period', *Biblical Archaeologist* 60.1, 2-51.

Bickerman, E. J., 2011. 'The God of the Maccabees', in A. Tropper (ed.), *Studies in Jewish and Christian History*, Leiden: E. J. Brill = Bickermann, E., 1937. *Der Gott der Makkabäer, Untersuchungen über Sinn und Ursprung der makkabäischen Erhebung*, Berlin: Schocken Verlag.

Bobota, V., 2013. *The Institution of the Hasmonean High Priesthood* (Supplements to the Journal for the Study of Judaism 165), Leiden / Boston: Brill.

Bowersock, G. W., 1983. *Roman Arabia*, Cambridge, MA: Harvard University Press.

Collins, J. J., and Sterling G. E., (eds.), 2001. *Hellenism in the Land of Israel* (Christianity and Judaism in Antiquity 13), Notre Dame, IN: University of Notre Dame Press.

Cotton, H. M., and Wörrle, M., 2007. 'Seleukos IV to Heliodoros. A new dossier of royal correspondence from Israel,' *ZPE* 159, 191–205.

Droysen, H., 1888. 'Die balustrade Reliefs' in Bohn, R., and Droysen, H., *Altertümer von Pergamon, band 2: Das Heiligtum der Athena Polias Nikephoros*, Berlin: W. Spemann, 93-138.

Fedak, J., 1990. *Monumental Tombs of the Hellenistic Age: A Study of Selected Tombs from the Pre-Classical to the Early Imperial Era*, Toronto: University of Toronto Press.

Fischer, M. L., and Tal, O., 2003. 'Architectural decoration in ancient Israel in Hellenistic times – some aspects of hellenisation', *Zeitschrift des Deutschen Palästina-Vereins*, 119.1, 19-37.

Fischer, T., 1990. 'Hasmoneans and Seleucids: aspects of war and policy in the second and first centuries B.C.E.', in A. Kasher, U. Rappaport and G. Fuks (eds.), *Greece and Rome in Eretz Israel, Collected Essays*, Jerusalem: Yad Izhak Ben-Zvi / Israel Exploration Society.

Fischer, T., and Anderson, H., 1992. 'Books of the Maccabees', in D. N. Freedman (ed.), *The Anchor Bible Dictionary*, Vol. 4. 439–454, New York: Doubleday.

Fontanille, J.-P., and Lorber, C., 2008. 'Silver Yehud coins with Greek and pseudo-Greek inscriptions', *Israel Numismatic Research* 3, 45-50.

Fleischer, R., 1996. 'Hellenistic royal iconography on coins,' in P. Bilde et al. (eds.), *Aspects of Hellenistic Kingship* (Studies in Hellenistic Civilization 7), Aarhus Univeristy Press: Aarhus, 96-116.

Fleischer, R., 1986. 'Die Tyche des Demetrios I von Syrien', *Archäologischer Anzeiger*, 699-706.

Geller, M. J., 1991. 'New information on Antiochus IV from Babylonian astronomical diaries,' *Bulletin of SOAS* 54.1, 1-4.

Gera, D., 2009. 'Heliodoros, Olympiodoros, and the Temples of Koilê Syria and Phoinikê', *Zeitschrift für Papyrologie und Epigraphik* 169, 125-155.

Gera, D., 1998. *Judaea and Mediterranean Politics 219 to 161 B.C.E.* (Brill's Series in Jewish Studies 8), Leiden / New York / Köln: Brill.

Gera, D., 1990. 'On the credibility of the history of the Tobiads (Josephus, Antiquities 12, 155-222)', in , in A. Kasher, U. Rappaport and G. Fuks (eds.), *Greece and Rome in Eretz Israel, Collected Essays*, Jerusalem: Yad Izhak Ben-Zvi / Israel Exploration Society.

Gitler, H., and Lorber, C., 2006. 'A new chronology for the Ptolemaic coins of Judah', *AJN Second Series* 18, 1-41.

Grainger, J. D., 2010. *The Syrian Wars* (Mnemosyne Suppl. 320), Leiden / Boston: Brill.

Grainger, J. D., 2002. *The Roman War of Antiochos the Great* (Mnemosyne Suppl. 289), Leiden / Boston: Brill.

Grainger, J. D., 1991. *Hellenistic Phoenicia*, Oxford: Clarendon Press.

Grainger, J. D., 1990. *The Cities of Seleukid Syria*, Oxford: Clarendon Press.

Gruen, E., 1998. *Heritage and Hellenism: The Reinvention of Jewish Tradition*, Berkeley / Los Angeles: University of California Press.

Gruen, E., 1976. 'Rome and the Seleucids in the aftermath of Pydna', *Chiron* 6, 73-95.

Habicht, C., 1976. 'Royal documents in Maccabees II', *Harvard Studies in Classical Philology* 80, 1-17.

Harlan, M., 1995. *Roman Republican Moneyers and Their Coins, 63 B.C.-49 B.C.*, London: Seaby / B. T. Batsford.

Hendin, D., 2007-2008. 'Numismatic expressions of Hasmonaean sovereignty', *Israel Numismatic Journal* 16, 76-91.

Houghton, A., 1992. 'The revolt of Tryphon and the accession of Antiochos VI at Apamea', *Schweizerische Numismatische Rundschau* 71, 119-141.

Houghton, A., 1983. *Coins of the Seleucid Empire from the Collection of Arthur Houghton* (Ancient Coins in North American Collections 4), New York: American Numismatic Society.

Hoover, O. D., 2007. *Coins of the Seleucid Empire from the Collection of Arthur Houghton*, Part 2 (Ancient Coins in North American Collections 9), New York: American Numismatic Society.

Hoover, O. D., 2007a. 'Revised Chronology for the Late Seleucids at Antioch (121/0-64 BC)', *Historia* 65.3, 280-301.

Hoover, O. D., 2005. 'Eleazar Auaran and the elephant: killing symbols in Hellenistic Judaea', *Scripta Classica Israelica* 24, 35-44.

Hoover, O. D., 2003. 'The Seleucid coinage of John Hyrcanus I: the transformation of a dynastic symbol in Hellenistic Judaea', *AJN Second Series* 15, 29-39.

Hoover, O. D., Houghton, A., and Veselý, P., 2008. 'The silver mint of Damascus under Demetrius III and Antiochus XII (97/6 BC-83/2 BC)', *AJN Second Series* 20, 305-36.

Huth, M., Potts, D. T., and Hoover, O. D., 2002. 'Laodice IV on the bronze coinages of Seleucus IV and Antiochus IV', *AJN Second Series* 14, 81-87.

Ilan, T., 1987. 'The Greek names of the Hasmonaeans', *Jewish Quarterly Review* 78, 1-20.

Isaac, B., 1991. 'A Seleucid Inscription from Jamnia-on-the-Sea: Antiochos V Eupator and the Sidonians,' *Israel Exploration Journal* 41, 132-144.

Jacobson, D. M., 2014. 'Herodian bronze and Tyrian silver coinage', *Zeitschrift des Deutchen Palästina-Vereins* 130.2, 138-154 and Tafs. 15-18.

Jacobson, D. M., 2013a. 'The lily and the rose: a review of some Hasmonean coin types', *Near Eastern Archaeology* 76.1, 16-27.

Jacobson, D. M., 2013b. 'Military symbols on the coins of John Hyrcanus I', *Strata: Bulletin of the Anglo-Israel Archaeological Society* 31, 43-56.

Jacobson, D. M., 2007. *The Hellenistic Paintings of Marisa* (PEF Annual 7), Leeds: Maney

Jacobson, D. M., 2007a. 'Who was "BACCHIVS IVDAEVS?"', *Numismatic Circular* 115.5, 256-257.

Jacobson, D. M., 2000. 'The anchor on the coins of Judaea', *Bulletin of the Anglo-Israel Archaeological Society* 18, 73-81.

Kasher, A., 1990. *Jews and Hellenistic Cities in Eretz-Israel* (Texte und Studien zum Antiken Judentum 21), Tübingen: J. C. B. Mohr.

Kindler, A., 2000. 'The Hellenistic influence on the Hasmonean coins', *Transactions of the International Numismatic Congress* 12, 316-323.

Landau, Y., 1966. 'A Greek inscription found near Hefzibah,' *Israel Exploration Journal* 16, 54-70.

Leibner, U., 2009. *Settlement and History in Hellenistic, Roman and Byzantine Galilee: An Archaeological Survey of Eastern Galilee*, Tübingen: Mohr Siebeck.

Ma, J., 1999. *Antiochos III and the Cities of Western Asia Minor*, Oxford: Oxford University Press.

McLean, M. D., 1981. 'The initial coinage of Alexander Jannaeus', *American Numismatic Society Museum Notes (ANSMN)* 26, 153-161.

Meshorer, Y., Bijovsky, G., and Fischer-Bossert, W., 2013. *Coins of the Holy Land: The Abraham and Marian Sofaer Collection at the American Numismatic Society and Israel Museum* (Ancient Coins in North American Collections 8), 2 vols., ed. D. Hendin and A. Meadows, New York: American Numismatic Society.

Millar, F., 1987. 'The problem of Hellenistic Syria,' in A. Kuhrt and S. Sherwin-White (eds.), *Hellenism in the East: The Interaction of Greek and Non-Greek Civilizations from Syria to Central Asia after Alexander*, London: Duckworth, 110-133.

Mørkholm, O., 1966. *Antiochus IV of Syria* (Classica et Mediaevalia, Dissertationes 8), Copenhagen: Gyldendalske-Nordisk.

Netzer, E., 2001. *Hasmonaean and Herodian Palaces at Jericho, Final Reports of the 1973-1987 Excavations*, Vol. I: *Stratigraphy and Architecture*, Jerusalem: Israel Exploration Society / Institute of Archaeology, Hebrew University of Jerusalem.

Noy, I., 2012. 'The victory wreath of Hyrcanus I', *Israel Numismatic Research* 5, 31-42.

Ostermann, S., 2005. *Die Münzen der Hasmonäer. Ein kritischer Bericht zur Systematik und Chronologie*, Göttingen: Vandenhoeck & Ruprecht.

Piccirillo, M., and Alliata, E., (eds.), 1999. *The Madaba Map Centenary 1897-1997, Travelling through the Byzantine Umayyad Period. Proceedings of the International Conference Held in Amman, 7-9 April 1997* (SBF Collectio Maior 40), Jerusalem: SBF.

Rahmani, L. Y., 1967. 'Jason's Tomb,' *Israel Exploration Journal* 17, 61-100.

Rajak, T., 1996. 'Hasmonean kingship and the invention of tradition', in P. Bilde et al. (eds), *Aspects of Hellenistic Kingship* (Studies in Hellenistic Civilization 7) Aarhus Univeristy Press: Aarhus, 96-116 = Rajak, T., 2001, *The Jewish Dialogue with Greece and Rome. Studies in Cultural and Social Interaction*, Leiden / Boston / Köln: Brill, 39-60.

Rajak, T., 1990. 'The Hasmonaeans and the uses of Hellenism', in P. R. Davies and R. T. White (eds.), *A Tribute to Geza Vermes: Essays on Jewish Literature and History* (JSOT Supplement Series 100), 261-280.

Rappaport, U. 2007. 'I Maccabees', in J. Barton and J. Muddiman (eds.), *The Oxford Bible Commentary* (2nd edn.), Oxford: Oxford University Press, 711-734.

Rappaport, U., 1992. 'Hellenization of the Hasmoneans,' in M. Mor (ed.), *Jewish Assimilation, Acculturation and Accommodation: Past Traditions, Current Issues and Future Prospects*, Lanham, NB: University Press of America, 1-13.

Rappaport, U., 1976. 'The emergence of Hasmonean coinage', *AJS Review* 1, 171-186.

Regev, E., 2013. *The Hasmoneans: Ideology, Archaeology, Identity* (Journal of Ancient Judaism. Supplements, 10), Göttingen: Vandenhoeck & Ruprecht.

Ronen, Y., 2003-2006. 'Some observations on the coinage of Yehud', *Israel Numismatic Journal* 15, 28-31.

Rosenberg, S. G., 2006. *Airaq al-Amir: The Architecture of the Tobiads* (BAR International Series 1544), Oxford: John and Erica Hedges.

Schwartz, D. R., 2008. *2 Maccabees. Commentaries on Early Jewish Literature*, Berlin / New York: Walter de Gruyter.

Schwartz, D. R., 2000. 'Antiochus IV in Jerusalem', in *Historical Perspectives: From the Hasmoneans to Bar Kokhba in Light of the Dead Sea Scrolls, Proceedings of the Fourth International Symposium of the Orion Center, 27-31 January 1999*, ed. D. Goodblatt, A. Pinnick and D. R. Schwartz, Lieden / Boston / Köln: Brill, 45-56.

Schwartz, S., 1998. 'The Hellenization of Jerusalem and Shechem', in M. Goodman (ed.), *Jewsin a Graeco-Roman World*, Oxford: Clarendon Press.

Seager, R., 2002. *Pompey the Great: A Political Biography*. Oxford: Blackwell Publishing.

Shatzman, I., 1991. *The Armies of the Hasmonaeans and Herod: From Hellenistic to Roman Frameworks* (Texte und Studien zum Antiken Judentum 25), Tübingen: J. C. B. Mohr, 1-125.

Sherwin-White, S. M., and Kuhrt, A., 1993. *From Samarkhand to Sardis: A New Approach to the Seleucid Empire*, Berkeley / Los Angeles: University of California Press.

Sievers, J., 2001. *Synopsis of the Greek Sources for the Hasmonean Period: 1-2 Maccabees and Josephus, War 1 and Antiquities 12-14* (Subsidia Biblica, 20), Rome: Pontifical Biblical Institute.

Stewart, A., 2014. *Art in the Hellenistic World: An Introduction*, Cambridge: Cambridge University Press.

Tal, O., 2012. 'Greek coinages of Palestine', in W. Metcalfe (ed.), *The Oxford Handbook of Greek and Roman Coins*, Oxford: Oxford University Press, 252-274.

Taylor, M. J., 2014. 'Sacred plunder and the Seleucid Near East', *Greece and Rome (2nd Series)* 61.2, 222-241.

Vermes, G., *The True Herod*, London / New York: Bloomsbury T & T Clark.

Waywell, G. B., and Berlin, A., 2007. 'Monumental tombs from Maussollos to the Maccabees', *Biblical Archaeology Review* 33.3, 54-65.

Will, E., and Larché, F., 1991. *Iraq al-Amir: Le château du Tobiade Hyrcan* (2 vols.), Paris: P. Geuthner.

STEMMATAS

SELEUCIDS

* Alexander *Balas* was the pretended or illegitimate son of Antiochus IV
** Alexander *Zabinas* may have been a son of Alexander *Balas*.

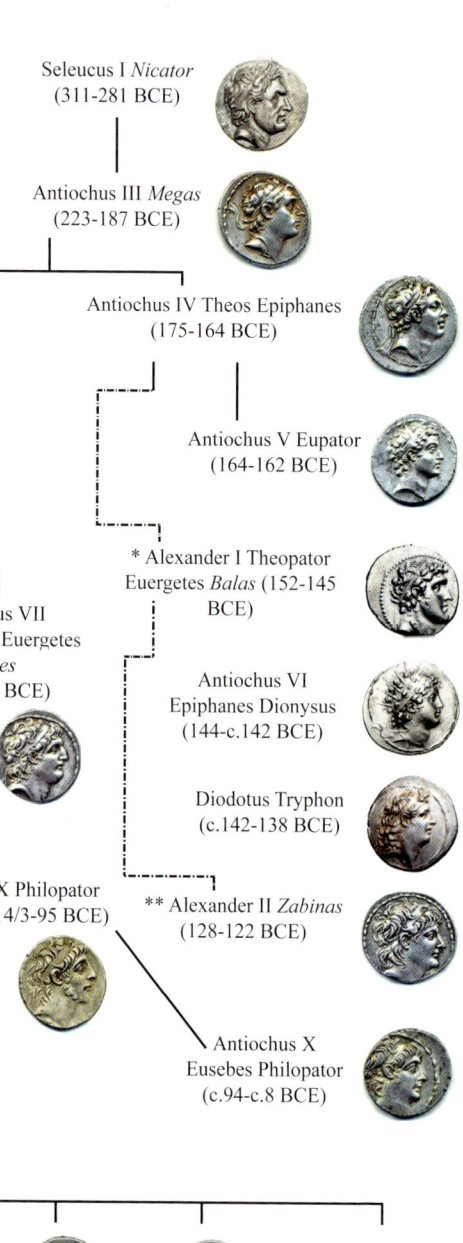

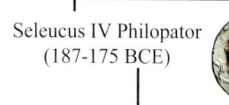

Seleucus I *Nicator* (311-281 BCE)

Antiochus III *Megas* (223-187 BCE)

Seleucus IV Philopator (187-175 BCE)

Antiochus IV Theos Epiphanes (175-164 BCE)

Antiochus

Antiochus V Eupator (164-162 BCE)

Demetrius I Soter (162-150 BCE)

* Alexander I Theopator Euergetes *Balas* (152-145 BCE)

Demetrius II Theos Philadelphos Nicator (146-138 BCE)

Antiochus VII Megas Soter Euergetes *Sidetes* (138-129 BCE)

Antiochus VI Epiphanes Dionysus (144-c.142 BCE)

(129-126/5 BCE)

Diodotus Tryphon (c.142-138 BCE)

Antiochus IX Philopator *Cyzicenus* (114/3-95 BCE)

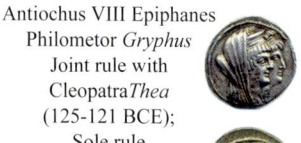

** Alexander II *Zabinas* (128-122 BCE)

Antiochus VIII Epiphanes Philometor *Gryphus* Joint rule with Cleopatra*Thea* (125-121 BCE); Sole rule (121/0-97/6 BCE)

Antiochus X Eusebes Philopator (c.94-c.8 BCE)

Seleucus VI Epiphanes Nicator (c.96- 94 BCE)

Antiochus XI Epiphanes Philadelphus (c.94/3 BCE)

Demetrius III Philopator Soter *Eucaerus* (97/6- 88/7 BCE)

Philip I Ephiphanes Philadelphus (c.95/4-c.76/5 BCE)

Antiochus XII Dionysus Epiphanes Philopator Callinicus (87/6-83/2 BCE)

166   ANTIOCH AND JERUSALEM

MACCABEES/HASMONAEANS

Mattathiah (to 166 BCE)

Judah
(166-161/60 BCE)

Jonathan
(161/60-143 BCE)

Simon
(143-135 BCE)

John *Hyrcanus* I
(135-104 BCE)

Judah Aristobulus I
(104-103 BCE)

Alexander Jannaeus
(103-76 BCE)